THE HANDBOOK OF AN AMBASSADOR OF THE KING

L'appel divin et le rôle de chaque croyant

Dr Jean Héder Petit-Frère

THE HANDBOOK OF AN AMBASSADOR OF THE KING

Copyright © 2025 by Dr. Jean Héder Petit-Frère

All rights reserved.

No part of this publication may be reproduced, stored in a retrieval system, or transmitted in any form or by any means—electronic, mechanical, photocopying, recording, or otherwise—without the prior written permission of the author, except in the case of brief quotations embodied in critical articles or reviews.

All Scripture quotations, unless otherwise indicated, are taken from the New King James Version®, copyright © 1982 by Thomas Nelson. Used by permission. All rights reserved.

Edited and compiled in collaboration with: Wadner Vilier

Jean Héder Petit-Frère International

ISBN (Hardback): 978-1-7346914-9-8

For more resources, teachings, and Kingdom training,

visit: www.jhpetitfrere.com

All rights reserved worldwide.

Table of Content

Author's Note	2
Foreword	4
Acknowledgments	6
Introduction: The Call to Represent the King	8
Disclaimer	10
Chapter 1	15
The Need for a Paradigm Shift	15
Introduction	16
The Nature of the Kingdom of God	16
The Paradigm Shift	17
A Paradigm Shift That Changes Everything	21
Understanding Governance: Kingdom vs. Democracy vs. Republic	21
Kingdom Governance: A Divine Paradigm	23
The Contrast Between a King, a President, and a Prime Minister	25
Conclusion	26
Chapter 2	28
The King and His Kingdom	28
Introduction	29
A Story Woven Through Time	29
The Creation Mandate	29
The Attributes of God as King	34
The Restoration of the Kingdom	35

The Nature of the Kingdom	36
Living as Kingdom Citizens	37
Conclusion	38
Chapter 3	40
The Divine Calling of an Ambassador	40
Introduction	41
The Role of a Kingdom Ambassador	41
Carrying the Message of the Kingdom	41
Chosen by the King	42
To reconcile the world to God.	44
The Responsibilities of an Ambassador	44
Building Relationships	45
Defending the interests of the kingdom	45
Access to Kingdom Resources	46
Challenges in Ambassadorship	46
Conclusion	47
Chapter 4	49
Protocol: The Framework for Effective Ambassadorship	49
Introduction	50
Defining Protocol in Diplomacy	50
Why Protocol Matters for Kingdom Ambassadors	50
The Consequences of Ignoring Protocol	51
Kingdom Ambassadors	52
Conclusion	53
Chapter 5	54

Reestablishing Diplomatic Relations Between Heaven and Earth 54

Introduction 55
The Fall: Humanity's Broken Relationship with Heaven 55
The Disruption of Sin 55
Jesus Christ: The Ultimate Emissary of Reconciliation 56
The Ministry of Reconciliation 57
Diplomatic Protocol for Kingdom Ambassadors 58
The Power of Reconciliation 59
Bringing Heaven to Earth 60
Conclusion 61

Chapter 6 62
The Ekklesia -
A Kingdom Nation in Action

62

Introduction 63
The Mission of the Ekklesia 63
The Authority of the Ekklesia 65
The Ekklesia in Action 66
Unity within the Ekklesia 67
Conclusion 67

Chapter 7 69
Kingdom Influence in Every Sphere of Society 69
Introduction 70
The Seven Pillars of Society 70

Understanding the culture	74
The Difference Between the Earth and the World	75
Practical Strategies for Influence	75
The role of Ekklesia in society	76
Conclusion	76
Chapter 8	78
Operating as Kingdom Diplomats in Modern Times	78
Introduction	79
The Nature of Modern Diplomacy	79
Characteristics of a Kingdom Diplomat	81
Engaging modern systems with kingdom influence	82
The Role of Prayer in Diplomacy	84
Overcoming Cultural Barriers	85
Conclusion	86
Chapter 9	87
Reflecting Heaven's Government in All Areas of Life	87
Introduction	88
Righteousness, Justice, Mercy, And Truth Characterize	88
Living Under Heaven's Government	89
Transforming Earthly Systems with Kingdom Principles	90
The Ekklesia's Role in Governance	92
Challenges in Reflecting Heaven's Government	93
Conclusion	94
Chapter 10	95
Walking in Kingdom Authority and Power	95

Introduction	96
The Source of Kingdom Authority	96
Operating in Kingdom Authority	98
Demonstrating the Power of the Kingdom	100
The Pitfalls of Misusing Authority	101
Releasing Heaven on Earth	102
Conclusion	102
Chapter 11	104
Building Bridges—Kingdom Expansion in Every Sphere	104
Introduction	105
The purpose of building bridges	105
The Role of Ambassadors in Kingdom Expansion	107
Demonstrating Kingdom Values	107
Strategies for effective bridge-building	108
Challenges in Building Bridges	110
The impact of kingdom expansion	111
Conclusion	112
Chapter 12	114
Challenges and Triumphs in the Ambassadorial Journey	114
Introduction	115
Challenges Faced by Kingdom Ambassadors	115
Strategies for Overcoming Challenges	118
The triumphs of Kingdom Ambassadors	120
The Eternal Perspective	121
Conclusion	122

Chapter 13	124
Living the Call: Transforming the World as Heaven's Representatives	124
Introduction:	125
The High Calling of Ambassadorship	125
The Impact of a Faithful Ambassador	127
The Eternal Perspective	128
The Legacy of an Ambassador	129
Bibliography	131
Final Note from the Author	133

Author's Note

Increasing chaos, brokenness, and a longing for identity and meaning characterize the world we live in today. Nations tremble under the weight of corruption, families crumble, and individuals grapple with despair. Yet, amid this confusion, there is a divine call—a call to rise above the turmoil and represent the one true King.

As a believer, your life is neither random nor purposeless. God's eternal plan intricately weaves your life. God has not merely saved you to escape the world's challenges, but to engage with them, bringing Heaven's transformative influence into every sphere of life. This is your Kingdom assignment.

This manual is more than a book; it is a roadmap, a training guide for stepping into your God-ordained role as an ambassador of the King. Drawing from years of personal experience, biblical study, and divine inspiration, I have sought to capture the essence of what it means to represent Heaven on Earth.

The Church is undergoing a profound shift, transitioning from traditional paradigms to becoming the Ekklesia governing body of Kingdom citizens who legislate Heaven's will on Earth. This book is a vital resource for equipping you to navigate this transformation, empowering you to engage with the world as a trans-dimensional ambassador of the Kingdom.

I pray that reading these pages will ignite your heart with passion, illuminate your mind with understanding, and equip your life for impactful Kingdom representation. Let us rise together as a kingdom nation, reflecting the glory, justice, and love of our King.

Dr. Jean Heder Petit Frère

Foreword

I am honored to have the privilege of providing the foreword for a true Kingdom Ambassador and Missionary Statesman Extraordinaire - Dr. Jean Heder Petit Frere.

This publication carries a most urgent assist to those desiring to usher Kingdom influence wherever their mission may be established and/or in progress.

A well-crafted handbook is beneficial to organizations and individuals by clarifying expectations, policies and procedures, promoting consistency, and ensuring compliance with Kingdom Covenant details.

In this treatise of diplomatic practicalities, Dr. Petit Frere provides an unfettered pathway to effective application of the principles of Kingdom Ambassadorship.

Among the many benefits this volume provides to its reader's are the following:

- Clarity and Understanding
- Access to Key References
- Enhancement of Critical Communication Skills
- A Sense of Empowerment for the Mission
- Insightful Meaning of Kingdom Culture
- Help to Minimize and Mitigate Conflict

It is clear that Dr. Petit Frere conveys a sense of urgency to all who undertake the Great Commission as mandated by the King of Kings and Lord of Lords, the Lord Jesus Christ.

Diplomacy is an art, a necessity, and a responsibility.

This handbook is a most helpful chart to assist the Ambassador of the King to navigate the vicissitudes typically encountered in diplomatic exchanges and pursuits. The reader and practitioner of the inspiring instructions within these pages will discover and appreciate the principle that communication is the basis of life. (Matthew 4:4)

Dr. Joseph M. Ripley
Pastor, Author, Ambassador

Acknowledgments

This book represents years of prayer, study, and a personal journey toward understanding and embracing the Kingdom of God. This book is a manifestation of love and a contribution to the Body of Christ. I owe a tremendous debt of gratitude to the individuals who have profoundly impacted my life and ministry.

First and foremost, I give thanks to my Lord and King, Jesus Christ, whose calling, grace, and empowerment have made this work possible. To Him be all the glory, honor, and praise.

I wish to pay a very special tribute to the late Dr. Myles Munroe, a true pioneer of the Kingdom awakening movement. His unparalleled ability to clarify and expound on the principles of the Kingdom of God and the concept of purpose became the signature of his life's work. Dr. Munroe's teachings continue to inspire countless lives, including my own, and his legacy serves as a guiding light for the Body of Christ to embrace the Kingdom message in its fullness.

Additionally, I extend heartfelt gratitude to the late Dr. Richard Pinder. His unwavering support in facilitating the Kingdom teachings and his personal investment in my life as a spiritual father have left an indelible mark on my journey. Dr. Pinder, your wisdom, mentorship, and kindness continue to echo in my heart. I still miss you deeply.

To my beloved wife, Marcia Elaine Petit Frère, your steadfast love, encouragement, and partnership have been my greatest earthly support. You are a gift from God, and I am forever grateful for your faithfulness and strength.

To my three Godly children, who exemplify the Kingdom values I hold dear: you inspire me daily with your faith and dedication.

To the faithful members of the Ekklesia I serve, your commitment to advancing the Kingdom has been a source of strength and encouragement. This book aims to further equip you for your mission as the hands and feet of Christ.

Finally, to my mentors, colleagues, and every believer who has prayed for, supported, or encouraged me along the way: this work is as much yours as it is mine.

May this book inspire, challenge, and equip every reader to step boldly into their divine calling as ambassadors of the King.

To all of you: thank you!

Introduction: The Call to Represent the King

What does it truly mean to be an ambassador? The term often conjures images of diplomats sent to foreign lands, representing the interests of their homeland. While this is accurate, the role of a Kingdom ambassador is far more profound and eternal.

The sovereign chooses, appoints, and sends an ambassador with the authority to act on their behalf. This calling for believers stems from our citizenship in the Kingdom of Heaven. Our mission transcends earthly borders, as we represent Heaven's culture, values, and authority wherever we go.

God's intention when creating humanity was clear: to establish His Kingdom on Earth as a reflection of Heaven's glory and governance. However, through sin, humanity severed its diplomatic relationship with Heaven, forfeiting its authority and plunging the world into darkness. In response, God, in His infinite love, sent Jesus Christ as the ultimate emissary to restore this connection.

Today, as Kingdom ambassadors, we carry the mantle of Jesus' mission. Our task involves representing the King, advancing His Kingdom, and transforming the world's systems to align with Heaven's culture. This calling encompasses not only church walls and religious activities, but also every sphere of life, including government, business, education, media, family, and more.

This handbook helps you activate your ambassador role, not just understand it. It's about moving from passive Christianity to active Kingdom engagement. Whether you are a teacher shaping the next generation, an entrepreneur influencing the marketplace, or a parent raising Kingdom-minded children, your role is vital. The Kingdom of God is not a distant future reality—it is a present reality, advancing through the lives of His ambassadors.

The journey ahead will make you rethink your identity, purpose, and mission. It will equip you with the tools to step boldly into your role as a representative of the King, bringing Heaven's transformative influence into a world desperate for hope and redemption. Are you ready to embrace the high calling of ambassadorship? The King is calling, and the world is waiting!

Disclaimer

"You have to study Kingdom in order to understand the Bible."

"The Bible contains religion, but it is not about religion."

"God did not give us the Bible to establish a religion, but to expand his kingdom on earth."

"God's ideal form of government is a kingdom where He is King."

CHAPTER 1

The Need for a Paradigm Shift

Introduction

The concept of God's Kingdom has long been central to Christian theology and spirituality.

It represents a paradigm shift that radically transforms how people view their lives, relationships, and purpose.

The Kingdom of God is more than just a distant and mystical concept.

It is a current reality that necessitates a fundamental reorientation of values and priorities.

This handbook will investigate the transforming nature of the Kingdom of God, looking at the implications for personal and communal life, as well as the impact on societal structures.

The Nature of the Kingdom of God

People frequently refer to the Kingdom of God as both a present reality and a hope for the future.

It is God's rule breaking into the earth, disrupting the status quo, and introducing a new way of life.

This dual aspect—already and not yet—creates a dynamic tension that drives believers to continue growing and evolving.

Present Reality

Jesus Christ's teachings and actions demonstrate the current actuality of the Kingdom of God. Through His parables, miracles, and encounters with people, Jesus demonstrated Kingdom ideals such as love, justice, mercy, and humility.

He invites you to experience the Kingdom in your daily lives by aligning with these principles and participating in God's redemptive activity in the world.

Manifestation

The Kingdom of God also symbolizes a promise of a time when God's dominion will fully manifest and all creation will return to its original balance.

This eschatological dimension gives Christians a feeling of purpose and direction, urging them to stay strong in their faith and work toward the ultimate completion of God's plan.

The Paradigm Shift

The Kingdom of God requires a paradigm shift that transforms everything.

This transformation entails transitioning from a self-centered to a God-centered viewpoint, from individualism to community, and from temporal concerns to eternal ideals.

From self-centered to God-centered

In a culture that usually values personal accomplishment and self-actualization, the Kingdom of God necessitates a significant turn toward God and His purposes.

This shift requires accepting God's sovereignty and striving to align one's life with His will.

It requires putting faith in God's provision and guidance rather than relying solely on one's own abilities and resources.

Individualism to Community
The Kingdom of God also changes how people interact with one another. It contradicts the dominant culture of individualism and promotes a community way of life.

In the Kingdom, relationships are defined by mutual love, respect, and support.

Believers are called to bear each other's burdens, share their resources, and work together for the greater good.

Temporal Concerns and Eternal Values
Finally, the Kingdom of God transfers the emphasis from temporal to everlasting values.

It encourages believers to live with an eternal perspective, valuing things of long-term value.

This entails valuing people over stuff, integrity over accomplishments, and service above power.

It entails fostering values like faith, hope, and love that last beyond the transitory moments of this life.

Implications in Personal Life
The Kingdom of God's paradigm shift has far-reaching consequences for personal existence. It shapes an individual's identity, purpose, and daily conduct.

Identity

In the Kingdom of God, identity is based on one's relationship with God.

Believers are considered God's children, adored and respected for who they are rather than what they do.

This concept of identity fosters a sense of worth and dignity, freeing people from the need to seek validation from external sources.

Purpose

The Kingdom of God gives believers a sense of purpose that goes beyond personal ambition.

It invites them to participate in God's redemptive activity in the world, utilizing their gifts and talents to help others and advance God's kingdom.

This purpose provides direction and meaning, inspiring people to live with intention and devotion.

Daily Conduct

The Kingdom of God's ideals impact our daily lives in practical ways.

In their interactions with others, believers should show compassion, justice, and mercy.

Impact on Social Structures

The Kingdom of God has significant implications for societal structures.

It opposes unfair structures and promotes a more egalitarian and caring society.

Justice
Justice is vital to the Kingdom of God. It entails not only dealing with individual acts of crime but also tackling structural injustices that marginalize and oppress.

God's kingdom ideals of preserving the rights and dignity of people, particularly the impoverished and disenfranchised, clearly align with the expectation for believers to fight for justice in all facets of life.

Compassion
Compassion is another essential value of the Kingdom of God. It requires a strong sense of empathy and care for the suffering of others.

This compassion goes beyond feeling to concrete actions that alleviate pain and promote well-being.

It entails developing methods and structures that facilitate the thriving of all members of society.

Peace
The Kingdom of God promotes peace, not just as the absence of conflict but as the presence of harmony and wholeness.

Reconciliation and the rebuilding of relationships lead to this peace.

We call believers to be peacemakers, striving to mend divisions and construct bridges of understanding and cooperation.

A Paradigm Shift That Changes Everything

Imagine a world in which there is no election, dispute, or deposition of the highest authority.

This is the reality Jesus invites us into when He says, "Repent" (Matthew 4:17).

The Kingdom of God is more than a spiritual catchphrase; it is a way of life that challenges traditional government systems such as democracy, republicanism, and even presidency.

Jesus is not a politician to vote for or criticize.

He is a King with absolute authority, possessing everything and expecting perfect obedience.

To understand His Kingdom, we must renounce democratic norms and embrace a paradigm shift.

Understanding Governance: Kingdom vs. Democracy vs. Republic

Kingdom Governance
A kingdom runs fundamentally differently than any modern governing system. Let us break it down:

Absolute Rule
The King's word is the law, and his decrees are binding. The King does not go to a vote or need approval.

Inheritance

Inheritance is the transmission of power by hereditary or divine right, symbolizing stability and continuation.

Ownership

Unlike presidents and prime ministers, who oversee people's lands, a monarch owns everything—land, resources, and even his subjects. Psalm 24:1 underscores this truth: "The earth is the Lord's, and everything in it."

God's rule as King is perfect and just, unlike worldly kings who frequently fail.

Psalm 10:16 and Exodus 15:18 are two examples of scripture that declare His perpetual kingship.

Isaiah 9:6-7 and Revelation 19:16, which refer to Jesus as the "King of Kings," fulfill prophecies about divine kingship.

Democratic Governance

- In contrast, democracy is about shared power and collective decision-making.
- Source of Authority: Power comes from the people, through elections.
- Accountability: Leaders hold temporary positions and are subject to removal.

Rights-Based System:

- Democracy prioritizes individual freedom and equality, making it inherently human-centered.
- While democracy is effective in human governance, its

instability (subject to public opinion) and fragmented authority often lead to inefficiency.

Republican Governance
A republic blends democracy with constitutional frameworks:

- Representation: Citizens elect leaders to govern on their behalf.
- Checks and Balances: The division of power among branches prevents tyranny.
- Rule of Law: A constitution safeguards individual rights.

However, like democracy, a republic is fallible, limited by the imperfections of human systems.

Kingdom Governance: A Divine Paradigm
In God's Kingdom, He centralizes authority rather than delegating or fragmenting it. This creates profound differences that demand a paradigm shift:

Comparison Table: Democratic Ideals vs. the Kingdom of God

Democratic Ideal	Kingdom Truth
Ownership vs. Stewardship	
We own our possessions.	All we "own" is God's, and we are stewards.
Rights vs. Submission	
We demand our rights.	We surrender our rights to follow the King's will.
Temporal vs. Eternal Authority	
Democratic Ideal	Kingdom Truth

Leaders serve for a limited time.	God's rule is eternal and unchanging.
Collective Rule vs. Sovereign Rule	
Power is distributed.	God, whose justice is perfect, holds all power.
Repentance	
Embracing a Kingdom Mindset requires a shift from democratic ideals to align with the eternal truths of God's Kingdom.	Embracing a Kingdom Mindset.

The word "repent" (Greek: metanoia) means to change one's mind.

Jesus isn't just asking us to feel sorry for our sins; He's calling us to rethink everything—our allegiance, our priorities, and our understanding of authority.

It's not about fitting the Kingdom into our lives but transforming our lives to align with the Kingdom.

Reflection Questions:
- What cultural mindsets about governance might you need to let go of?
- How can you surrender autonomy to embrace submission to the King?

The Contrast Between a King, a President, and a Prime Minister

"For the LORD is our judge, the LORD is our lawgiver, the LORD is our king; it is He who will save us." (Isaiah 33:22)

Understanding the Kingdom of God requires a clear grasp of how it differs from worldly governance systems. This is particularly crucial because the democratic principles familiar to most are often in stark contrast to the realities of Kingdom rule.

Below is an in-depth comparison of the roles of a king, a president, and a prime minister.

A King

Source of Authority

A king's authority is absolute and inherent, not derived from the people or elections. It is based on divine or hereditary rights.

In contrast, the authority of a president or prime minister stems from democratic systems, making it conditional and temporary.

Ownership

In a kingdom, the king owns everything—land, resources, and even the people, who are considered his subjects.

Biblical Comparison: Psalm 24:1 emphasizes, "The earth is the Lord's, and everything in it," reflecting the total ownership by the King.

A president or prime minister acts merely as a steward, with ownership belonging to the people or the state.

Law

The king's word is law—unchallenged, permanent, and not subject to debate or approval.

> **Example:** God's decrees are eternal and unchangeable, underscoring His ultimate sovereignty.

However, presidents and prime ministers operate within structures where laws undergo debate, amendment, and voting.

Conclusion

A king rules with total sovereignty, and the king's character shapes the nature of the kingdom.

A just king establishes a just kingdom; a corrupt king leads to oppression.

By comparison, a president or prime minister operates within checks and balances, distributing authority and often limiting their impact.

> **Examples:**

God as King: Scripture highlights God's eternal kingship and perfect authority (Exodus 15:18, Psalm 93:1-2).

Jesus as King: Jesus fulfills His role as the eternal King, sovereign over God's Kingdom (Isaiah 9:6-7, John 18:36-37).

Reflection Questions:

1. Does understanding the King's character affect your view of your role in the Kingdom?
2. In what ways can you bring the culture of Heaven into your daily life?
3. Reflect on the areas of your life where the King's authority

is not fully evident. What steps can you take to align them with His rule?

CHAPTER 2

The King and His Kingdom

Introduction

The story of God's Kingdom is a timeless narrative of divine love, sovereignty, and restoration.

From the Creation Mandate in Genesis to the eternal reign in Revelation, it reveals God's ultimate plan to establish His rule on Earth. God gave humanity the privilege of stewardship, created in His image, but sin disrupted this divine purpose. Yet, God's response through Jesus Christ demonstrates His unwavering commitment to redemption and restoration.

By understanding the Kingdom of God and the Kingdom of Heaven, believers can embrace their role as ambassadors of Heaven on Earth.

This exploration invites us to align our lives with the King's values and fulfill our calling in His eternal Kingdom.

A Story Woven Through Time

The Bible tells a continuous story of a King and His Kingdom, spanning from Genesis to Revelation. This divine narrative reveals God's eternal plan to establish His rule on Earth—a kingdom reflecting His glory, character, and authority.

The Creation Mandate

God intended for the Earth to be a realm where He expressed and carried out His divine will, creating it as an extension of Heaven.

Made in God's image, humanity was tasked to govern Earth as His representatives, stewards, and mirrors of His glory.

The Disruption of Sin

Through disobedience, humanity severed its relationship with God, introducing sin and disrupting the divine order.

This act displaced humanity from its intended purpose, allowing darkness and rebellion to influence the Earth.

God's Response
The Eternal Kingdom: Despite mankind's rebellion, God's Kingdom remains eternal and unshaken.

The Plan of Redemption Through Jesus Christ, God initiated a redemptive plan, calling believers to carry out the Kingdom mission and reestablish His rule on Earth.

Is There a Difference Between the Kingdom of God and the Kingdom of Heaven?
The terms "Kingdom of God" and "Kingdom of Heaven" appear frequently in Scripture, leading to questions about their meaning and whether they refer to the same concept or have distinct differences.

A closer look at the Bible reveals both similarities and differences, shaped by the context of the terms.

The Similarities
Both the Kingdom of God and the Kingdom of Heaven originate from God and reflect His sovereign rule and authority.

Scriptures like Matthew 19:23-24 use the terms interchangeably.

"It is hard for a rich man to enter the Kingdom of Heaven... It is easier for a camel to go through the eye of a needle than for a rich man to enter the Kingdom of God."

God's Sovereign Reign
Both terms describe the rule and reign of God over all creation, emphasizing submission to His authority and alignment with His divine will.

Same Invitation
Whether referred to as the Kingdom of God or the Kingdom of Heaven, the invitation is for believers to enter through repentance, faith, and obedience to Jesus Christ (Matthew 4:17; Mark 1:15).

Key Distinctions
While the Kingdom of God and the Kingdom of Heaven overlap in meaning, their usage reflects distinct emphases in Scripture:

Terminology Usage:
- The Gospel of Matthew exclusively uses the term "Kingdom of Heaven" (e.g., Matthew 3:2; Matthew 5:3; Matthew 13:24).
- The term "Kingdom of God" appears across the Gospels, Acts, and epistles, indicating a broader usage (e.g., Mark 1:15; Luke 17:21; Romans 14:17).

Audience Sensitivity
Matthew, writing primarily to a Jewish audience, often avoids using the word "God" out of reverence, instead substituting "Heaven" to respect Jewish sensitivities. Thus, "Kingdom of Heaven" aligns with Jewish customs, while the "Kingdom of God" would resonate with a Gentile or broader audience.

Heavenly vs. Universal Scope

The Kingdom of Heaven often emphasizes the realm of God's rule and reign from a heavenly perspective, reflecting God's sovereignty as it manifests on Earth.

The Kingdom of God highlights the universal nature of God's dominion over all creation, not limited to Heaven but extending into every aspect of life.

Examples of the Difference:

Heaven's Reign on Earth (Kingdom of Heaven):

This term encapsulates the reality of believers establishing God's heavenly authority on Earth as they carry out His will. For instance, the Beatitudes (Matthew 5:3-12) illustrate the principles of Heaven manifested in human lives.

God's Rule Over All Creation (Kingdom of God):

This term encompasses a broader view, including the spiritual transformation of individuals and communities under God's rule, as described in Romans 14:17: "For the Kingdom of God is not eating and drinking, but righteousness and peace and joy in the Holy Spirit."

Are They the Same or Different?

Both terms describe God's rule and reign, whether on Earth or universally. They point to the same reality of submission to God's authority and participation in His divine mission.

The nuances in their usage reflect differences in emphasis:

- "Kingdom of Heaven" highlights God's heavenly authority

and its expression on Earth.

- "Kingdom of God" underscores the universal and spiritual dimension of His rule.

Why Does This Matter?

Understanding the subtle differences aids believers in better interpreting passages that use these terms and understanding their cultural and theological context.

Living the Kingdom Mission

Both the heavenly principles of the Kingdom of Heaven (living as reflections of God's will) and the universal mission of the Kingdom of God (bringing transformation to every sphere of life) are required of believers.

Reflection Questions:

1. When you hear "Kingdom of Heaven" or "Kingdom of God," how do you perceive their significance in your life?
2. How can understanding these terms deepen your participation in God's Kingdom mission on Earth?
3. Are there specific areas where you can better reflect Heaven's culture or God's universal rule in your daily walk?

The Centrality of the King

The King Defines the Kingdom.

A kingdom cannot exist without a king. Unlike earthly systems such as democracies or republics, a kingdom is defined by the governing influence of a king over his territory.

Key Characteristics of a Kingdom

- Legislative bodies, not the King's will and purpose, govern.
- The King's desires are manifested within His domain (Matthew 6:10).

The Attributes of God as King

God owns all creation, including His people (Deuteronomy 10:14; Psalm 24:1).

> ***Example:*** Just as a landlord holds rights over a property, God holds authority over His Kingdom.

Sovereignty

God's authority is eternal and unmatched (Psalm 103:19).

His decrees are final, reflecting His unchangeable rule.

Justice

God is a righteous judge who ensures fairness (Psalm 89:14).

He defends the oppressed and upholds truth.

Love and Mercy

Unlike earthly rulers, God reigns in compassion, offering grace to His subjects (Psalm 86:15).

Provision

God meets the needs of His people, providing spiritual and material blessings (Philippians 4:19).

The Kingdom Mandate

The Original Mandate
Genesis 1:26: God created humanity to rule Earth, reflecting his justice, peace, and prosperity.

Humanity's Fall

Adam and Eve's disobedience handed authority to darkness, but God's plan did not end.

The Restored Mandate
According to Romans 5:17, Jesus Christ restores believers to their position as stewards of God's Kingdom.

> *Example:* Imagine a CEO reinstating a disqualified manager, trusting them to restore order and efficiency.

The Restoration of the Kingdom

Jesus' Proclamation
"Repent, for the Kingdom of Heaven is at hand" (Matthew 4:17).

The Invitation
Jesus called humanity to reenter God's original design through repentance and transformation.

The Role of Jesus
As Heaven's ultimate ambassador, Jesus reconciled humanity to God, restoring Kingdom relations.

Think of an ambassador sent to repair relations between two nations. Jesus bridged the gap between God and humanity. Today, believers continue this mission, representing the King as Kingdom ambassadors.

The Nature of the Kingdom

Unseen Yet Powerful
The Kingdom exists within the hearts of believers (Luke 17:21).

> **Example:** Like wind shaping the landscape, the Kingdom's influence is invisible but transformative.

Already and Not Yet
The Kingdom is present wherever God's will is done but will only be fully realized upon Christ's return (Daniel 7:27).

Inclusive
Open to all who accept the King, transcending earthly divisions (Galatians 3:28).

Accessible Yet Demanding
It is freely offered but requires surrender and commitment (Matthew 16:24).

Everlasting
Unlike earthly kingdoms, God's Kingdom is eternal (Daniel 7:14).

Transformational
Wherever it establishes itself, it brings justice, restoration, and life (Colossians 1:20).

Countercultural

It values humility and sacrificial love over power and pride (John 13:15).

Living as Kingdom Citizens

Kingdom Citizenship
Citizenship in God's Kingdom is not a physical birthright but a spiritual transformation (Colossians 1:13-14).

Characteristics of Kingdom Citizens
- Allegiance to the King: Seek first the Kingdom in all aspects of life (Matthew 6:33).
- Transformed Identity: Embrace the identity of being children of God (Romans 8:17).
- Adherence to Kingdom Laws: Live by principles of love, grace, and justice (Matthew 22:37-39).

Representation
Act as Christ's ambassadors, reflecting the King's character (2 Corinthians 5:20).

Living as Light
Illuminate the world with Kingdom values (Matthew 5:14).

Privileges of Kingdom Citizenship
- Prayer provides direct access to the King.
- Divine protection and provision.
- Eternal security in God's promises.

Practical Steps to Live as Kingdom Citizens

Seek First the Kingdom
Prioritize God's will in all decisions.

> **Example:** Before making financial decisions, align plans with Kingdom values.

Represent the King
Reflect Christ's character in daily interactions.

> **Example:** Show integrity and compassion in the workplace.

Engage the World
Influence society with Kingdom principles.

> **Example:** Volunteer in community programs, embodying Christ's love.

Conclusion

The King invites every believer to participate in His redemptive mission. This is not merely a theological concept but a practical reality. The King calls us to bring Heaven's culture to Earth.

Reflection Questions
1. Can you change your life to reflect Kingdom values?
2. How can you influence your family, workplace, or community with Kingdom principles?
3. In what areas of your life can you seek the King's will more intentionally?

CHAPTER 3

The Divine Calling of an Ambassador

Introduction

An ambassador's role is one of profound importance. As representatives of their sovereign, ambassadors embody the authority, character, and values of the kingdom they serve.

For believers, this calling extends to every aspect of life, from personal interactions to systemic influence.

Paul declares:

"We are therefore Christ's ambassadors, as though God were making His appeal through us" (2 Corinthians 5:20, NKJV).

Our mission as Kingdom ambassadors is to represent Heaven's culture, advance its agenda, and reflect on the King in everything we do.

The Role of a Kingdom Ambassador

Representation of the King

Ambassadors are the face of their king to the world. Every spoken word and action taken reflects on the King they serve.

> ***Example:*** In a workplace setting, treating colleagues with respect and fairness demonstrates the King's love and justice, even in challenging environments.

Carrying the Message of the Kingdom

We entrust ambassadors with the Gospel—the message of reconciliation, hope, and transformation. This message is central to their mission.

Biblical Foundation

"He has committed to us the message of reconciliation" (2 Corinthians 5:19, NKJV).

> **Example:** Sharing your testimony with someone who is seeking purpose or struggling with hopelessness becomes a tangible way to carry the Kingdom message.

Advocacy and diplomacy

Ambassadors build bridges between the Kingdom of God and the systems of the world. They advocate for righteousness and justice, often standing in the gap to mediate and reconcile.

> **Example:** Organizing a community initiative to address social injustice or inequity demonstrates advocacy aligned with Kingdom values.

Chosen by the King

God has handpicked each believer for a specific purpose. The King does not appoint ambassadors arbitrarily. He sees beyond human limitations, recognizing the potential within each of His children to fulfill their divine assignment.

> ***BiblicalExample:*** Gideon

Gideon's story in the Bible illustrates the transformative power of God's calling. Despite seeing himself as the least in his family and belonging to the weakest clan, God chose Gideon to deliver Israel from the Midianites. When the angel of the Lord appeared to him, he said:

"The Lord is with you, mighty man of valor!" (Judges 6:12, NKJV).

As he embraced his calling and relied on God's strength, Gideon's initial hesitation gave way to boldness.

Consider areas in your own life where you feel unqualified or inadequate. Remember, the King's calling equips you with what seems impossible. Your weaknesses become a platform for His strength.

Appointed for a Purpose
God's calling always serves a purpose. Our role as Kingdom ambassadors is to influence the world for the King.

To represent the King
Our primary purpose is to reflect the King's nature and values in every aspect of our lives. This involves living in a way that points others to God's love, grace, and holiness.

> ***Example:*** A business leader who models ethical practices, generosity, and fairness reflects the King's character in a sector often dominated by greed and corruption.

To Advance the Kingdom
The mission of ambassadors is to bring Heaven's culture to Earth by influencing society with the values of justice, righteousness, and peace.

> ***Example:*** In a community struggling with violence, an ambassador might organize initiatives promoting reconciliation and youth empowerment, transforming the atmosphere through Kingdom values.

To reconcile the world to God.

Reconciliation is at the heart of an ambassador's mission. Ambassadors carry this message, inviting humanity back into relationship with God through Christ.

Biblical Foundation:
"Now all things are of God, who has reconciled us to Himself through Jesus Christ and has given us the ministry of reconciliation" (2 Corinthians 5:18, NKJV).

> ***Example:*** Sharing your testimony with someone who feels distant from God can spark their journey toward reconciliation.

The Responsibilities of an Ambassador

Living in alignment with Kingdom Values
The Kingdom holds ambassadors to its standards. Their lives must reflect the principles of love, truth, humility, and holiness.

Choosing to act with integrity in a business deal, even when it may result in personal loss, aligns with Kingdom values and builds credibility.

Engaging with World Systems
Despite not belonging to the world, ambassadors have a responsibility to interact with it. This means influencing government, education, business, and other systems to reflect Kingdom principles.

> ***Biblical*** Example: Daniel

Despite serving in a pagan government, Daniel remained faithful to God, influencing policies and decisions that brought glory to the King of Heaven.

Building Relationships

Influence often begins with relationships. Ambassadors must be intentional about fostering trust and connection with those around them.

> **Example:** Mentoring a young person in your community can plant seeds of Kingdom influence that grow far beyond your immediate reach.

Defending the interests of the kingdom

Ambassadors protect and advocate for the Kingdom's values and interests, even in hostile environments.

> **Biblical** Example: Esther

Esther risked her life to advocate for her people, using her position of influence to protect the interests of God's covenant nation.

The Privileges of Ambassadorship

Authority of the King

Ambassadors operate under the authority of the sovereign they represent. This grants them the ability to act boldly and confidently in their mission.

Biblical Foundation

"I have given you authority to trample on snakes and scorpions and to overcome all the power of the enemy" (Luke 10:19, NKJV).

> **Example:** Praying for healing or deliverance with confidence, knowing that you carry the authority of the King.

Access to Kingdom Resources

Ambassadors have access to the full resources of their homeland, equipping them to fulfill their mission.

> ***Example:*** When faced with financial or logistical challenges in ministry, trusting in God's provision often creates unexpected opportunities.

Protection from the King

Just as a nation protects its ambassadors, the King shields those who serve Him faithfully.

Biblical Foundation:

"The Lord will fight for you; you need only to be still" (Exodus 14:14, NKJV).

Challenges in Ambassadorship

Opposition from the World

Ambassadors often face resistance from systems and individuals who oppose the values of the Kingdom.

Biblical Foundation:

"If the world hates you, keep in mind that it hated Me first" (John 15:18, NKJV).

> ***Example:*** Standing for ethical practices in a corrupt business environment may invite criticism or alienation, but it reflects Kingdom integrity.

Maintaining Integrity in a Hostile Culture

Ambassadors must resist the temptation to conform to worldly values, remaining steadfast in their identity and mission.

Biblical Foundation:
"Do not conform to the pattern of this world but be transformed by the renewing of your mind" (Romans 12:2, NKJV).

Practical Steps for Ambassadors
Study the King's Decrees Immerse yourself in Scripture to understand the principles and values of the Kingdom.

Rely on the Holy Spirit
Depend on the Spirit's guidance to navigate complex situations and represent the Kingdom effectively.

Model Kingdom Values
Let your life be a living testimony of the Kingdom's principles, inspiring others to follow.

Conclusion
Ambassadors reflect the King's character through their actions, carry the message of the Gospel, and influence systems with Kingdom values.

Reflection Questions
1. How can you better align your life with the values of the Kingdom?

2. How can you overcome your problems representing the King?

3. What practical steps can you take today to influence your sphere with Kingdom principles?

CHAPTER 4

Protocol: The Framework for Effective Ambassadorship

Introduction

Protocol is an essential aspect of ambassadorship, both in earthly diplomacy and the Kingdom of God. It refers to the formal rules and principles that govern interactions, ensuring respect, order, and alignment with the sovereign's authority.

Defining Protocol in Diplomacy

In the diplomatic world, protocols govern how ambassadors engage with leaders, participate in official ceremonies, and conduct themselves in foreign nations. It ensures that their actions honor their sovereignty and maintain the dignity of their office.

Defining Protocol in the Kingdom

In the Kingdom, protocol reflects the divine order and principles established by God. It governs how ambassadors approach the King, interact with others, and carry out their mission.

Kingdom protocol goes beyond rules to reflect the King's character and will.

Why Protocol Matters for Kingdom Ambassadors

- Following protocol safeguards the mission, preventing actions that could harm relationships or misrepresent the Kingdom.
- It ensures alignment with the king's will.
- Adherence to protocol keeps ambassadors in sync with the King's purposes, releasing His favor and blessing.
- It builds trust and credibility.
- Respecting protocol earns ambassadors the trust of their targets and the King's approval.

Protocol in Action: Biblical Examples

Esther and the Persian King
Esther respected the court protocol of approaching the king only when summoned. By preparing through fasting and prayer and acting with wisdom and humility, she gained the king's favor and saved her people.

"If I perish, I perish." (Esther 4:16, NKJV)

David and the Ark of the Covenant
When David first attempted to transport the Ark, he ignored God's protocol, resulting in Uzzah's death. Following God's instructions and correcting his approach, the mission succeeded, bringing the Ark to Jerusalem with great joy.

"When those who were carrying the Ark of the Lord had taken six steps, he sacrificed a bull and a fattened calf." (2 Samuel 6:13, NKJV)

Jesus' submission to the Father
Jesus perfectly adhered to Kingdom protocol, always seeking the Father's will and acting in alignment with His purposes. This submission was the foundation of His ministry's power and success.

"I do nothing on my own but speak just what the Father has taught me." (John 8:28, NKJV)

The Consequences of Ignoring Protocol

Loss of credibility and influence
Disregarding protocol damages relationships and undermines the

ambassador's mission.

Disorder and chaos
Protocol provides structure and clarity. Ignoring it leads to confusion and inefficiency.

Divine Judgment and Discipline
Biblical examples, such as the deaths of Nadab and Abihu, show that ignoring God's instructions can lead to severe consequences.

Kingdom Ambassadors

Study and understand protocols
Ambassadors must immerse themselves in God's Word, seeking to understand the principles that govern their mission.

Rely on the Holy Spirit
The Holy Spirit provides guidance and discernment, enabling ambassadors to navigate complex situations while adhering to protocol.

Model Integrity and Excellence
Following protocol not only benefits the ambassador but also sets an example for others, inspiring trust and respect.

Demonstrate humility and submission
Protocol begins with a heart of humility and a willingness to submit to the King's authority.

Conclusion
Protocol is not a burden but a tool that empowers ambassadors

to represent the King effectively. It reflects the order and wisdom of God, ensuring that His ambassadors operate with integrity, credibility, and success.

By respecting protocol, Kingdom ambassadors honor their King, protect their mission, and position themselves for divine favor.

Reflection Questions

1. How can you deepen your understanding of Kingdom protocols?
2. Are there areas where you have neglected or misunderstood protocol?
3. Can you change your behavior to follow the King?
4. Where are you already a Kingdom ambassador?
5. How can you better align your character with the King you represent?
6. What steps can you take to engage with the world and advance the Kingdom's agenda?

CHAPTER 5

Reestablishing Diplomatic Relations Between Heaven and Earth

Introduction

From the moment God created humanity, there was a divine relationship between Heaven and Earth. God tasked humanity with stewardship, reflecting His character and carrying out His will on Earth. However, sin disrupted this connection, creating a chasm between Heaven and Earth.

But the story does not end there. God's plan of redemption, through Jesus Christ, reestablished diplomatic relations, inviting humanity back into fellowship with Him. Our mission as Kingdom ambassadors is to restore this connection, both spiritually and practically.

The Fall: Humanity's Broken Relationship with Heaven

The Original Design

God created humanity in His image, commissioning Adam and Eve to govern the Earth as His representatives. God gave them dominion and called them to cultivate the Earth according to Heaven's principles (Genesis 1:26-28).

Practical Insight

Humanity's role was not to dominate the Earth for selfish gain but to steward it with love, reflecting God's character.

The Disruption of Sin

When Adam and Eve disobeyed God, they forfeited their authority and broke the relationship between Heaven and Earth. Sin introduced chaos, corruption, and separation.

Consequences:

- Loss of Dominion: Humanity surrendered its authority to the enemy.
- Separation from God: Fear and shame replaced intimacy with God (Genesis 3:8-10).
- Corruption of Creation: The Earth, once a reflection of Heaven, became subject to decay and destruction (Romans 8:20-22).

God's Response

Despite humanity's failure, God initiated a plan of reconciliation. He promised a Redeemer who would restore the connection between Heaven and Earth (Genesis 3:15).

Jesus Christ: The Ultimate Emissary of Reconciliation

Reestablishing Diplomatic Relations

The Father sent Jesus as the ultimate ambassador to restore the lost. Through His life, death, and resurrection, He bridged the gap between Heaven and Earth.

Biblical Foundation:

"For God was pleased to have all His fullness dwell in Him, and through Him to reconcile to Himself all things" (Colossians 1:19-20, NKJV).

The Message of Reconciliation

Jesus proclaimed the Kingdom of God, inviting humanity to return to fellowship with the Father. His message was one of hope, restoration, and transformation.

> **Example:** Through acts of healing, forgiveness, and compassion, Jesus demonstrated the reality of Heaven's culture on Earth.

The Victory of the Cross
At the cross, Jesus defeated sin, death, and the powers of darkness, restoring humanity's authority to operate as Kingdom ambassadors.

Biblical Foundation:
"God made Him who had no sin to be sin for us, so that in Him we might become the righteousness of God" (2 Corinthians 5:21, NKJV).

The Ministry of Reconciliation

Our Role as Ambassadors
Restoring relationships with God

Our primary mission is to lead others into reconciliation with God. This involves sharing the Gospel, discipling believers, and modeling a life that reflects the love and holiness of the King.

Organizing a community outreach event that caters to both physical and spiritual needs can provide opportunities for individuals to encounter God's love.

Reconciling Communities
Kingdom ambassadors work to bring healing and unity to broken families, communities, and nations. This involves addressing social injustices, fostering forgiveness, and building bridges of

understanding.

> ***Example:*** Mediating a conflict within a family or organization can demonstrate the power of God's peace and reconciliation.

Transforming Systems
Beyond individual relationships, ambassadors are called to influence systems—government, education, business, and more—aligning them with Kingdom principles.

> ***Example:*** Advocating for policies that promote justice and equity within a local government reflects the values of Heaven.

Diplomatic Protocol for Kingdom Ambassadors
Effective ambassadors operate according to the King's principles and directives. Protocol ensures alignment with His will and maximizes the impact of their mission.

Maintain constant communication
Just as earthly diplomats stay in touch with their homeland, Kingdom ambassadors must maintain a close relationship with God through prayer, worship, and the study of His Word.

Biblical Foundation:
"Pray without ceasing" (1 Thessalonians 5:17, NKJV).

Operate with Integrity
Ambassadors must act with honesty and transparency, ensuring their actions reflect the values of the Kingdom.

> ***Example:*** Being truthful in your dealings, even when it may cost

you, upholds the integrity of the King's name.

Demonstrate Cultural Awareness
Effective ambassadors comprehend the culture and context of the people they serve. This allows them to communicate the Kingdom message in ways that resonate.

> ***Example:*** Using local traditions or stories to illustrate Gospel truths makes the message more relatable and impactful.

Advocate for Peace
Ambassadors are peacemakers, working to resolve conflicts and promote harmony. This includes standing against injustice and advocating for righteousness.

Biblical Foundation:
"Blessed are the peacemakers, for they will be called children of God" (Matthew 5:9, NKJV).

The Power of Reconciliation
Reconciliation is at the heart of the Kingdom mission. It brings healing, restoration, and transformation to every level of life.

Healing Broken Relationships
Whether between individuals, families, or communities, reconciliation restores what sin has fractured.

> ***Example:*** Counseling a couple on the brink of divorce can lead to restored love and unity, reflecting the redemptive power of the Kingdom.

Restoring Order to Systems

When we introduce Kingdom principles, we redeem corrupt systems and create environments where justice and righteousness thrive.

> ***Example:*** Partnering with organizations to address systemic poverty or inequality reflects Heaven's commitment to justice.

Bringing Heaven to Earth

Every act of reconciliation is a step toward the ultimate goal: the realization of Heaven on Earth.

Biblical Foundation:

"Your kingdom come, Your will be done, on Earth as it is in Heaven" (Matthew 6:10, NKJV).

Practical Steps for Ambassadors

- Pray for Reconciliation: Intercede for broken relationships, communities, and systems, asking God to bring healing and restoration.

- Engage with Intentionality: Look for opportunities to serve as a bridge between Heaven and Earth, whether through relationships, projects, or advocacy.

- Live as anExample: Model reconciliation in your own life by seeking forgiveness, extending grace, and building unity wherever possible.

- Equip Others: Train and empower others to join the ministry of reconciliation, multiplying your impact for the Kingdom.

Conclusion

The ministry of reconciliation is a sacred calling. As Kingdom ambassadors, we have the privilege and responsibility to restore the connection between Heaven and Earth, bringing healing, hope, and transformation.

The world is waiting for ambassadors who will rise to this challenge. Will you answer the call and step into your role as a bridge-builder for the Kingdom?

Reflection Questions

1. How can you actively participate in the ministry of reconciliation in your community?
2. Are there relationships in your life that need healing or restoration?
3. What steps can you take to influence systems around you with Kingdom principles?
4. What does reconciliation mean to you, and how can you participate in this ministry in your community?
5. Are there areas in your life where you need to restore your relationship with God or others?
6. How can you bring Kingdom values to the systems and structures you interact with daily?

CHAPTER 6

The Ekklesia - A Kingdom Nation in Action

Introduction

When Jesus said, "I will build My church, and the gates of Hades will not overcome it" (Matthew 16:18, NKJV), He introduced a revolutionary concept. The Greek word Ekklesia, which referred to an assembly of citizens called out to govern the affairs of a city-state, inspired the translation of the word "church". This assembly had the authority to legislate, make decisions, and shape the culture.

> **Jesus** redefined Ekklesia as a governing body of Kingdom citizens entrusted with advancing Heaven's agenda on Earth.

Ekklesia is not a building-bound religious institution, but a nation of ambassadors tasked with world transformation.

The Mission of the Ekklesia

The Ekklesia is not passive—it is active and transformational. Its mission includes the following:

Advancing the Kingdom Agenda

The Ekklesia's duties include establishing God's will in every area of life, influencing systems, transforming culture, and bringing Heaven's culture to Earth.

> **As** a Example, hosting community forums to address local issues while incorporating Kingdom principles can influence governance and policy.

Legislating in the Spirit

As a governing body, the Ekklesia has the authority to legislate in the spiritual realm. This includes prayer, intercession, and declarations that release Heaven's power.

Biblical Foundation:
"I will give you the keys of the Kingdom of Heaven; whatever you bind on Earth will be bound in Heaven, and whatever you loose on Earth will be loosed in Heaven" (Matthew 16:19, NKJV).

Disciplining Nations
The Great Commission calls the Ekklesia to disciple nations, teaching them to observe Christ's commands. This involves engaging with cultural, educational, and governmental institutions to align them with Kingdom values.

> ***Example:*** Developing leadership training programs that incorporate biblical principles equips future leaders to operate with integrity and wisdom.

The Ekklesia is Heaven's Embassy
Every nation has embassies in foreign lands, serving as extensions of their homeland's authority and culture. The Ekklesia functions as Heaven's embassy on Earth, a place where:

Kingdom culture is taught and demonstrated
The Ekklesia is a hub for discipleship, equipping believers to live out Kingdom values and principles.

> ***Example:*** Churches offering classes on financial stewardship, parenting, or ethical business practices reflect Heaven's priorities.

Kingdom resources are distributed
The Ekklesia provides spiritual resources—teaching, fellowship, and empowerment by the Holy Spirit—that equip believers for their mission.

Kingdom citizens find refuge
The Ekklesia is a sanctuary for those navigating the challenges of a broken world, offering encouragement, healing, and restoration.

The Authority of the Ekklesia
The authority of the Ekklesia is derived from the King. Jesus declared, "All authority in Heaven and on Earth has been given to Me" (Matthew 28:18, NKJV), and He entrusted this authority to His Ekklesia.

Binding and Loosing
The Ekklesia can bind and loosen things that go against Grace.

> ***Example:*** Interceding for a city plagued by violence and declaring peace and restoration through prayer demonstrates the power of binding and losing.

Speaking Truth to Power
Just as prophets in the Old Testament confronted kings, the Ekklesia is called to address corruption, injustice, and unrighteousness.

> ***Example:*** Advocating for ethical policies or calling for accountability in leadership aligns societal systems with Kingdom standards.

Declaring Heaven's Will
Through prayer and proclamation, the Ekklesia releases Heaven's agenda into the earthly realm.

Biblical Foundation:
"Your Kingdom come, Your will be done, on Earth as it is in

Heaven" (Matthew 6:10, NKJV).

The Ekklesia in Action

The Ekklesia is not confined to spiritual activities within church walls. We call the Ekklesia to engage with the world, bringing Kingdom influence into every sphere of society.

Government and leadership

The Ekklesia advocates for policies and leaders that align with Kingdom values, promoting justice and integrity.

> **Example:** Partnering with government officials to implement community development initiatives reflects Kingdom principles.

Business and economy

Kingdom entrepreneurs and professionals demonstrate ethical practices and create opportunities that reflect God's generosity.

Education

Believers in education shape the minds of future generations by challenging ungodly ideologies and promoting truth.

Media and Arts

Through storytelling and creative expression, the Ekklesia shapes cultural narratives, showcasing the creativity and redemption of the Kingdom.

Unity within the Ekklesia

For the Ekklesia to fulfill its mission, unity is essential. Division weakens its influence, while unity releases God's power.

One body and many parts
The Ekklesia is diverse, with each member bringing unique gifts and perspectives. All members must work together for the common mission.

Biblical Foundation:
"Now you are the body of Christ, and each one of you is a part of it" (1 Corinthians 12:27, NKJV).

Spiritual Alignment
Unity comes from aligning with the Spirit of God, focusing on His will rather than personal agendas.

Mutual Support
The Ekklesia calls its members to support and encourage one another, fostering a culture of love and collaboration.

> ***Example:*** Churches collaborating on city-wide outreach events demonstrate the power of unity in advancing the Kingdom.

Conclusion
The world is waiting for the Ekklesia to rise. The time for passive Christianity is over. The King is calling His people to step into their roles as Kingdom ambassadors and members of His governing body.

Reflection Questions
1. How do you see the role of the Ekklesia in your community or nation?
2. What steps can you take to contribute to the mission of the Ekklesia?
3. Does your life need to align more with Kingdom values and

missions?

CHAPTER 7

Kingdom Influence in Every Sphere of Society

Introduction

When Jesus commanded His disciples to "Go into all the world" (Mark 16:15, NKJV), He was commissioning them to engage with the systems, ideologies, and spheres that govern human life. These include government, education, business, family, media, arts, and more. His call extended beyond geographical boundaries, aiming to transform the very fabric of society.

As ambassadors of the Kingdom, our calling extends beyond personal holiness to include societal reformation. Matthew 5:13-16 sends us into these spheres as salt and light, infusing them with Heaven's culture and values, and ensuring the fulfillment of God's will "on Earth as it is in Heaven" (Matthew 6:10, NKJV).

The Seven Pillars of Society

The Seven Pillars are foundational areas that shape societies and determine their trajectory. Kingdom ambassadors hold a unique position to influence these spheres with divine principles, guaranteeing the triumph of God's purposes.

1. Government and Leadership

Governments shape laws, enforce justice, and determine the future of nations. This sphere is pivotal in ensuring peace, equity, and righteousness. Kingdom ambassadors bring integrity, accountability, and wisdom to this realm, advocating for policies and practices that honor God.

> ***Biblical*** Example: Joseph's leadership in Egypt not only preserved lives but also displayed God's wisdom to a pagan nation (Genesis 41).

> **Example:** A Christian serving in local government can push for ethical governance, transparency, and justice for the marginalized.

Reflection: How can you advocate for righteousness within your local governance structures?

2. Business and economics
The marketplace is a powerful force in distributing resources and shaping societal wealth. Kingdom ambassadors' model ethical practices, stewardship, and generosity, using their platforms to honor God and uplift communities.

> **Biblical** Example: The Proverbs 31 woman was a successful entrepreneur who provided for her family and gave to the needy.

> **Example:** Starting a business that champions fair wages and supports community initiatives reflects Kingdom values.

Marketplace leaders can integrate Kingdom principles into hiring practices, ensuring fair treatment of employees, and using profits to support Kingdom causes.

3. Education
Education molds the minds of future generations, influencing what they believe and how they act. Kingdom ambassadors in this sphere challenge ungodly ideologies, promote truth, and instill biblical values in students.

> **Example:** Teachers can subtly introduce biblical principles, such as integrity and perseverance, within the curriculum, creating a foundation for critical thinking rooted in truth.

Christian schools and educators can collaborate to design curricula that emphasize godly values and provide safe environments for learning.

4. Media and arts

Media and arts shape narratives, public opinion, and cultural values. Kingdom ambassadors use these platforms to highlight redemption, truth, and hope, pushing back against darkness.

> **Biblical** Example: David's Psalms are timeless artistic expressions of worship, connecting generations with God.
>
> **Example:** Producing a documentary on faith-based resilience during adversity can inspire viewers and shift cultural perceptions.

Musicians, filmmakers, and artists can intentionally create works that reflect God's creativity, influencing the culture positively.

5. Families and relationships

The family is God's first institution and the cornerstone of society. Healthy families lead to healthy communities. Promoting God's design for marriage, parenting, and relationships is the task of kingdom ambassadors.

> **Example:** Hosting workshops on building strong marriages or leading parenting classes grounded in biblical principles fosters healthier family dynamics.

Ministries can extend their focus to single-parent households and blended families, offering support and biblical guidance tailored to their unique challenges.

6. Health and well-being

Physical, emotional, and spiritual health are vital for flourishing communities. Kingdom ambassadors in this sphere bring compassion, healing, and holistic care, demonstrating God's concern for the whole person.

> ***Biblical*** Example: Jesus' healing ministry was a profound demonstration of Heaven's love for the broken.
>
> ***Example:*** Launching mobile health clinics that offer medical care alongside prayer and encouragement brings restoration to underserved areas.

Kingdom healthcare professionals can advocate for mental health awareness and integrate prayer and faith-based counseling in their practices.

7. Science, innovation, and agriculture

Innovation is a reflection of God's creativity. In this sphere, Kingdom ambassadors develop solutions that honor creation, improve lives, and steward resources wisely.

> ***Biblical*** Example: Bezalel and Oholiab's spirit-filled craftsmanship in designing the Tabernacle reflects the integration of divine creativity and skill (Exodus 31:1–6).
>
> ***Example:*** Launching eco-friendly agricultural initiatives that combat food scarcity while caring for creation reflects Kingdom stewardship.

Engaging the Spheres of Influence

Kingdom ambassadors must intentionally engage the systems of this world to effect change. Engagement involves preparation, collaboration, and perseverance.

Understanding the culture

An effective ambassador must study the values, needs, and dynamics of the sphere they are called to influence.

> **Example:** A teacher researching community education gaps can advocate for programs that align with biblical values.

Bringing Kingdom Principles

Introducing integrity, generosity, compassion, and justice into these spheres begins the transformation process.

Collaborating with others

Ambassadors cannot bring about societal reformation alone. Working together, leveraging gifts and networks, amplifies impact.

> **An** Example of this is when churches partner with businesses to address homelessness, combining spiritual guidance with practical resources.

Persevere in the Face of Opposition

Change is rarely easy, and ambassadors may face resistance. With perseverance, trust in God's timing, and reliance on the Holy Spirit, they can overcome challenges.

The Difference Between the Earth and the World

The Earth
The Earth, as God's creation, reflects His creativity and beauty. We, as Kingdom ambassadors, have a responsibility to responsibly steward it.

The World
The world refers to the systems and ideologies corrupted by sin. Our mission is to transform these systems to align with Kingdom principles.

Scriptural Mandate:
"Do not conform to the pattern of this world but be transformed by the renewing of your mind" (Romans 12:2, NKJV).

Practical Strategies for Influence

Start where you are
Recognize the influence you already have within your family, workplace, or community, and begin living out Kingdom values.

Build Relationships
Trust and collaboration form the foundation for effective change. Invest in relationships to create opportunities for dialogue and influence.

Pursing Excellence
Excellence glorifies God, garners credibility, and creates opportunities for influence.

Speaking Truth to Power
Ambassadors must be bold in advocating for righteousness, even

in the face of opposition.

Pray for transformation
Prayer invites God's power into broken systems and situations, aligning them with His will.

The role of Ekklesia in society

The Ekklesia is the engine behind societal transformation, equipping ambassadors to engage with the world effectively.

Equipping for Service
Training programs and discipleship initiatives prepare believers to impact their spheres of influence.

Mobilizing for Impact
The Ekklesia organizes collaborative efforts to tackle societal challenges, from education reform to poverty alleviation.

Advancing the Kingdom Agenda
As a unified body, the Ekklesia strategically influences nations to align with Christ's Kingdom.

Conclusion

The mission of Kingdom ambassadors is to transform the systems of the world with Heaven's principles and power. This calling requires faith, courage, and obedience, but it also brings the privilege of partnering with God to see His Kingdom established on Earth.

Wherever God has placed you, remember that your influence carries the authority of the King. The world is waiting for the light, hope, and truth you bring.

Reflection Questions

1. Which sphere of influence has God called you to engage with?
2. How can you apply Kingdom principles in your current context?
3. What steps can you take to build relationships and create change in your sphere?
4. Are there specific systems or ideologies you feel called to challenge or transform?
5. How can you collaborate with others to expand your kingdom's influence?

CHAPTER 8

Operating as Kingdom Diplomats in Modern Times

Introduction

A diplomat's role is critical: to represent their homeland, build alliances, and influence decisions in foreign lands. As ambassadors of the Kingdom, we embody the role of spiritual diplomats, serving as a conduit between Heaven and humanity.

Our mission involves introducing Kingdom values to a world often opposed to them, standing as beacons of hope and transformation.

In today's fast-paced and ever-changing world, this role demands a deep reliance on the Holy Spirit, cultural awareness, and practical wisdom.

Engaging with societal systems without conforming to them, Kingdom diplomacy seeks to influence them with the transformative power of God's Kingdom.

The Nature of Modern Diplomacy

Diplomacy involves navigating relationships, fostering collaboration, and bridging gaps between diverse perspectives. Kingdom diplomacy mirrors this by engaging with the world's systems while maintaining fidelity to God's principles.

Cultural Awareness

To influence effectively, ambassadors must understand the culture, beliefs, and values of those they seek to impact. Cultural sensitivity enhances communication and builds trust.

> **Biblical** Example: Paul in Athens connected with the Greeks by referencing their altar to an "unknown god," skillfully introducing the Gospel within their cultural framework (Acts 17:22–31).

> **Example:** A Christian social worker who takes into account cultural customs and traditions can effectively address community needs while introducing Kingdom values.

Cultural awareness also involves respecting traditions without compromising biblical truth. Attending a community festival presents a chance to discreetly and respectfully impart biblical principles.

Spiritual Discernment

The Holy Spirit is the ultimate guide for Kingdom ambassadors.
Discernment enables us to see spiritual realities behind physical situations and develop strategies aligned with God's will.

Scriptural Foundation:
"When He, the Spirit of truth, comes, He will guide you into all the truth" (John 16:13, NKJV).

> **Example:** A pastor leading a prayer walk in a neighborhood plagued by violence may discern specific spiritual strongholds to address, such as fear or despair, tailoring intercessory prayers accordingly.

Relational Intelligence
Trust is the currency of diplomacy.

Ambassadors must prioritize relationship-building, display empathy, understanding, and effective communication skills to foster collaboration and influence.

> **Example:** A Christian entrepreneur partnering with secular businesses to address societal challenges builds trust and opens avenues for Kingdom impact.

Relational intelligence includes active listening and meeting people where they are. Organizing interfaith dialogues on ethical business practices while subtly introducing Kingdom principles is one example.

Characteristics of a Kingdom Diplomat

Being a Kingdom diplomat requires spiritual fortitude and practical skills. These characteristics enable ambassadors to navigate challenges effectively while advancing God's agenda.

Wisdom and strategy

Diplomats must be strategic, navigating challenges with discernment. Jesus' instruction to be "wise as serpents and innocent as doves" (Matthew 10:16) captures the balance of shrewdness and purity required in diplomacy.

Strategy involves knowing when to speak boldly and when to observe quietly, always prioritizing the Holy Spirit's timing.

Patience and persistence

Kingdom transformation is a long-term process. Patience ensures that ambassadors remain faithful even when results are not immediate.

> **Example:** A missionary working in a resistant culture may spend years building trust before seeing fruit, but perseverance aligns them with God's timing.

Perseverance involves spiritual stamina, such as fasting and prayer, to break through resistance.

Courage and boldness

Representing the Kingdom often means standing firm against opposition, injustice, and cultural resistance. Ambassadors must have the courage to confront wrongs and speak truth in love.

> ***Biblical*** Example: The courage of Shadrach, Meshach, and Abednego to defy King Nebuchadnezzar's decree demonstrates bold allegiance to God over human authority (Daniel 3:16–18).
>
> ***Example:*** A believer opposing unethical practices in their workplace may risk alienation but demonstrates the power of standing for Kingdom principles.

Servant Leadership

Kingdom diplomats lead by serving others, reflecting Christ's humility and love. Their leadership inspires transformation by modeling God's heart.

> ***Biblical*** Example: Jesus washing His disciples' feet exemplifies servant leadership, demonstrating love, humility, and a willingness to serve others (John 13:1–17).
>
> ***Example:*** A community leader organizing food drives for the homeless embodies servant leadership, meeting practical needs while sharing God's love.

Engaging modern systems with kingdom influence

Kingdom ambassadors are not called to isolate themselves but to engage meaningfully with the systems of the world, bringing Heaven's influence into every sphere.

Government and policy

Ambassadors in government advocate for justice, equity, and righteousness, influencing policies to reflect Kingdom values.

> **Biblical** Example: During the famine, Joseph's leadership in Egypt preserved lives, demonstrating God's wisdom and compassion (Genesis 41).

A believer working in local government might champion initiatives to provide resources for underserved communities.

Business and innovation

Christian entrepreneurs can model ethical practices, provide fair wages, and use profits to benefit society, reflecting God's generosity.

> **Example:** A business donating a portion of its profits to community development projects reflects Kingdom stewardship.

Kingdom-minded business leaders can mentor young entrepreneurs, ensuring a legacy of integrity and innovation.

Education and knowledge

Educators shape the minds of the next generation. Christian teachers and administrators can embed biblical principles into curricula and foster environments of truth and integrity.

> **Example:** A Christian professor developing a course on ethics and

> morality incorporates biblical wisdom into academic discussions.

Hosting after-school programs that provide mentorship and discipleship can influence students' lives beyond the classroom.

Media and arts
Media and arts are powerful tools for shaping culture. Kingdom ambassadors use them to tell stories of redemption, justice, and hope, influencing public narratives.

> **Example:** Creating films or writing articles that emphasize faith-based resilience and social justice has the potential to influence cultural norms.

Visual artists creating murals with biblical themes in public spaces introduce Kingdom principles subtly into the cultural conversation.

The Role of Prayer in Diplomacy
Prayer is the foundation of spiritual diplomacy, aligning ambassadors with God's will and empowering them to operate in divine authority.

Releasing Heaven's will on earth
Prayers enable ambassadors to bring Heaven's solutions to Earth's problems. It's a powerful tool to release divine strategies.

Breaking Strongholds
Through prayer, Kingdom ambassadors can dismantle spiritual strongholds that hinder transformation.

> **Example:** Prayer teams interceding for cities with high crime

rates can target spiritual roots like greed, anger, and despair, paving the way for peace.

Interceding for Leaders
We call ambassadors to pray for leaders, asking God to guide their decisions and actions.

Scriptural Mandate:
"I urge, then, first of all, that petitions, prayers, intercession, and thanksgiving be made for all people—for kings and all those in authority." (1 Timothy 2:1–2, NIV).

Navigating Opposition and Resistance
Kingdom ambassadors face resistance, but grace and perseverance enable them to remain effective.

Responding to persecution
Ambassadors must respond to criticism or opposition with grace, trusting God to vindicate them.

Overcoming Cultural Barriers
Ambassadors bridge cultural gaps by demonstrating understanding and love, fostering trust and dialogue.

Maintaining Integrity
Staying faithful to Kingdom principles ensures long-term credibility and influence.

The impact of Kingdom Diplomacy
When ambassadors operate effectively, the results are transformative:

- Restored Relationships: Healing divides and fostering unity

- Systems Reformed: Influencing governance, business, and education with Kingdom principles.
- Community Revitalized: Bring healing, hope, and renewal.
- Nations Transformed: Fulfilling the Great Commission by discipling nations.

Conclusion

You, as Kingdom diplomats, bear the responsibility of representing Heaven. This role requires courage, humility, and a deep reliance on God. Step boldly into your assignment, knowing that the King empowers you to navigate challenges and transform the world.

Reflection Questions

1. In what areas of society can you serve as a Kingdom diplomat?
2. How can you build bridges in your community to share Kingdom values?
3. What steps can you take to influence systemic challenges where you are?
4. How can you use prayer to strengthen your impact as a Kingdom diplomat?
5. What personal qualities can you cultivate to become a more effective representative of Christ?

CHAPTER 9

Reflecting Heaven's Government in All Areas of Life

Introduction

The Kingdom of God operates on principles vastly different from the systems of this world. These principles serve as the blueprint for the functioning of life, relationships, and governance, not just as mere ideals. Our role as Kingdom ambassadors involves mirroring Heaven's governance in every aspect of our lives and guiding the surrounding systems to conform to God's plan.

Righteousness, Justice, Mercy, And Truth Characterize

Heaven's government. We must first live under the King's rule to embody His order, peace, and justice in our spheres of influence.

Understanding Heaven's Government

The Nature of Heaven's Rule

The nature and character of God form the foundation of Heaven's government. It stands in stark contrast to earthly systems often tainted by corruption and self-interest.

Justice and Righteousness Fairness and moral integrity form the foundation of God's rule.

Scriptural Foundation:

"Righteousness and justice are the foundation of Your throne; mercy and truth go before Your face" (Psalm 89:14, NKJV).

Mercy and Grace

The government of Heaven is redemptive, offering forgiveness and restoration.

> ***Example:*** An organization implementing restorative justice practices reflects Heaven's redemptive nature.

Peace and Order
Heaven's government replaces chaos with divine harmony and structure.

Scriptural Foundation:
"For God is not the author of confusion but of peace" (1 Corinthians 14:33, NKJV).

Truth and Transparency
Deception has no place in Heaven's government, which operates with unwavering honesty.

> ***Example:*** The principles of honesty and transparency in the workplace reflect those of Heaven's government.

The Role of the King
The Kingdom reflects the character of its King, who governs with absolute authority, unwavering love, and infinite wisdom.

Scriptural Foundation:
"The Lord reigns forever; He has established His throne for judgment. He rules the world in righteousness and judges the peoples with equity" (Psalm 9:7–8, NKJV).

Reflecting Heaven's government begins with acknowledging God's sovereignty in every decision and action.

Living Under Heaven's Government

Submitting to the King's Authority
Living under Heaven's government starts with full submission to God's rule, surrendering our desires to align with His will.

Scriptural Mandate:
"Your Kingdom come, Your will be done, on Earth as it is in Heaven" (Matthew 6:10, NKJV).

> **Example:** A leader who consults God in prayer before making major decisions serves as an example of submission to the King's authority.

Walking in obedience
Obedience to God's Word aligns our lives with the standards of Heaven. Through obedience, we become vessels for His plans and purposes.

> **Example:** Choosing integrity in business dealings, even when it results in personal loss, reflects Kingdom obedience.

Reflecting Kingdom Values
Ambassadors must embody Kingdom values such as love, humility, generosity, and integrity in their personal and professional lives.

> **Example:** A manager who treats employees with dignity and fairness demonstrates Heaven's principles in the workplace.

Transforming Earthly Systems with Kingdom Principles

We call Kingdom ambassadors to engage with and transform worldly systems, ensuring they reflect Heaven's values.

Government and leadership

Ambassadors advocate for justice, equity, and servant leadership within governance.

> ***Biblical*** Example: Nehemiah rebuilt Jerusalem's walls, uniting people and exemplifying godly leadership (Nehemiah 2–6).

A local leader prioritizing projects for underserved communities reflects Heaven's justice and compassion.

Business and economics

The marketplace is a platform for demonstrating stewardship, fairness, and generosity.

> ***Example:*** An entrepreneur who invests in sustainable practices and supports employee welfare reflects the justice and generosity of Heaven's government.

Businesses in the Kingdom can establish scholarship programs or initiatives to uplift marginalized communities.

Education and media

Ambassadors in education and media shape culture by teaching truth and communicating values that align with God's principles.

A teacher fostering respect and equity in the classroom helps create a culture reflective of Heaven's order.

A media producer incorporates Kingdom values into cultural narratives by creating content that fosters unity and hope.

The Ekklesia's Role in Governance

The Ekklesia is the governing body of Kingdom citizens, tasked with spiritual and practical governance on Earth.

Spiritual Legislation

Through prayer and intercession, the Ekklesia binds what opposes God's will and loses what aligns with His purposes.

Scriptural Mandate:

"Whatever you bind on Earth will be bound in Heaven, and whatever you loose on Earth will be loosed in Heaven" (Matthew 18:18, NKJV).

> ***Example:*** An intercessory prayer group focusing on systemic corruption can release divine wisdom and solutions into governance.

Modeling Kingdom Governance

The Ekklesia exemplifies unity, love, and accountability, offering a model for governance rooted in Heaven's values.

> ***Example:*** Churches collaborating to provide disaster relief demonstrate the efficiency and compassion of Heaven's government.

Raising Kingdom Leaders

Ekklesia equips believers to step into leadership roles across various spheres, ensuring Kingdom principles influence society.

Leadership training programs that combine spiritual formation with practical skills create a pipeline of Kingdom-minded influencers.

Challenges in Reflecting Heaven's Government

Cultural Resistance
The world often resists change, holding onto flawed systems and ideologies. Ambassadors must navigate these challenges with patience and wisdom.

Pressure to conform
Ambassadors may feel pressure to compromise their values for acceptance or success. Remaining steadfast requires courage and reliance on God.

Scriptural Encouragement:
"Do not conform to the pattern of this world, but be transformed by the renewing of your mind" (Romans 12:2, NIV).

Spiritual Opposition
Advancing Heaven's government invites spiritual warfare. Ambassadors must remain vigilant, using prayer and the Word of God as their weapons.

Practical steps for reflecting Heaven's government

- Lead by example: Ambassadors must model the values they wish to promote, demonstrating love, humility, and integrity.
- Engage with Systems: Active participation in societal systems allows ambassadors to influence policies and practices for Kingdom transformation.
- Equip and Disciple Others: Equipping others multiplies the

impact of kingdom principles, ensuring their reach in every sphere.

> **Example:** A mentoring program for young leaders fosters future Kingdom ambassadors in various fields.

- Persist in prayer: Prayer lays the foundation for transformation, releasing Heaven's authority into earthly systems.

> **Example:** A prayer group interceding for local leaders creates a spiritual atmosphere for righteous decision-making.

Conclusion

Reflecting Heaven's government is both a privilege and a responsibility. We, as Kingdom ambassadors, bear the responsibility of embodying the King's values and bringing transformation to the world's systems. The task may seem daunting, but with the King's authority and the Holy Spirit's power, transformation is not only possible but inevitable.

Reflection Questions

1. How can you align your life more fully with Heaven's government?
2. What specific systems or structures in your community could benefit from Kingdom transformation?
3. In what ways can you equip others to join in the mission of reflecting Heaven's rule?
4. What practical steps can you take today to influence your sphere with Kingdom principles?
5. How can you overcome challenges such as resistance or pressure to conform while maintaining your Kingdom values?

CHAPTER 10

Walking in Kingdom Authority and Power

Introduction

We carry the authority and power of Heaven to fulfill our divine mandate as Kingdom ambassadors. We carry the authority and power of Heaven to fulfill our divine mandate.

> **This** authority, given through Jesus Christ, enables us to advance the Kingdom, confront spiritual darkness, and release God's will on Earth.

However, this authority is not for personal gain or recognition. We entrust this authority to serve others, glorify God, and bring transformation wherever we go.

To walk effectively in this authority, we must understand our identity, align with God's purposes, and actively engage the systems of the world with faith and obedience.

When we operate in Kingdom authority, we become agents of change, bringing light to dark places, hope to the hopeless, and order to chaos.

The Source of Kingdom Authority

Authority originates from the King

Jesus is the ultimate source of all authority. He declared, "All authority in Heaven and on Earth has been given to Me" (Matthew 28:18, NKJV).

> **As** His ambassadors, we operate under His delegated authority. This means our power flows directly from Him, and we must remain submitted to His rule to exercise it effectively.

An ambassador's authority is valid only as long as they represent their sovereign faithfully. In the same way, our authority is effective when we remain aligned with Christ's will and purposes.

Authority through the Great Commission

The Great Commission in Matthew 28:19–20 entrusts believers with a clear mandate: to disciple nations, baptize new believers, and teach them to obey Christ's commands. This authority encompasses:

- Proclaiming the Gospel: Sharing the good news of salvation through Christ.
- Healing the Sick: Demonstrating the power of the Kingdom through physical restoration.
- Casting Out Demons: Liberating those oppressed by spiritual forces.
- Confronting Injustice: Standing against systems that perpetuate sin and oppression.

> **Example:** A believer notices an issue of inequality in their workplace and led by prayer, initiates a proposal for fairer practices, demonstrating the authority of Christ to challenge and correct injustice.

The Great Commission is not just about individual transformation but societal reformation. It calls us to influence communities, institutions, and nations with the culture of Heaven.

Empowerment by the Holy Spirit

Kingdom authority is impossible to wield effectively without the empowerment of the Holy Spirit. The Spirit equips believers with wisdom, boldness, and spiritual gifts, enabling them to fulfill their mission.

Scriptural Foundation:
"You will receive power when the Holy Spirit comes on you, and you will be My witnesses" (Acts 1:8, NKJV).

> ***Example:*** A pastor leading a revival meeting relies on the Holy Spirit's guidance to discern specific needs, pray for healing, and deliver anointed messages that transform lives.

Operating in Kingdom Authority

Know your identity.
Authority flows from identity. Being sons and daughters of the King changes how we handle challenges. Knowing who we are in Christ gives us confidence and boldness to exercise the authority He has entrusted to us.

Scriptural Mandate:
"The Spirit you received brought about your adoption to sonship" (Romans 8:15, NIV).

A teacher confident in their identity as a Kingdom ambassador integrates biblical values into lessons on ethics and morality, influencing students to embrace higher standards.

When believers grasp their identity, they no longer fear opposition or inadequacy. Instead, they walk with the assurance of divine backing.

Aligning with the King's Will

The exercise of authority must align with God's purposes. Ambassadors must seek discernment and remain obedient to God's instructions, ensuring their actions reflect His heart.

> ***Example:*** Before addressing a conflict in their community, a Kingdom ambassador spends time in prayer, asking for wisdom and direction from God.

Insight: Misaligned authority—acting without God's leading—can lead to frustration and failure. Submission to the King ensures our authority carries Heaven's full backing.

Declare Heaven's Will

Words carry creative power. Kingdom authority involves boldly declaring God's promises, rebuking injustice, and speaking life into situations.

Scriptural Mandate:

"Truly I tell you, if you have faith and do not doubt... you can say to this mountain, 'Go, throw yourself into the sea,' and it will be done." (Matthew 21:21, NIV).

> ***Example:*** During a community crisis, a prayer group declares peace, provision, and restoration over the affected areas, aligning their words with God's promises.

Declarations are not mere positive affirmations; they are acts of faith rooted in God's Word, releasing His power into the earthly realm.

Confrontation with Darkness

The Kingdom calls its ambassadors to combat spiritual and systemic darkness. This includes:

- Breaking strongholds through prayer.
- Standing against corruption and injustice.
- Setting captives free from oppression.

Scriptural Mandate:
"Submit yourselves to God. Resist the devil, and he will flee from you" (James 4:7, NIV).

> *Example:* A believer identifies a cycle of addiction in their community and initiates intercession for a breakthrough, while collaborating with organizations that offer practical support.

Demonstrating the Power of the Kingdom

Healing the Sick

Healing is a tangible demonstration of Heaven's authority over sickness and death. Jesus exemplified healing as a crucial component of His ministry, and we must emulate His example.

Scriptural Mandate:
"They will place their hands on sick people, and they will get well" (Mark 16:18, NIV).

A believer prays for a colleague battling illness, and the miraculous healing that follows leads to a conversation about faith.

Delivering the Oppressed

Deliverance is a powerful testimony of Christ's victory over spiritual forces. We must equip ambassadors to confront demonic oppression and bring freedom.

> ***Example:*** A youth leader, discerning spiritual oppression in a student's life, prays with authority, breaking chains and restoring peace to the individual.

Performing Miracles

Miracles confirm God's presence and validate the authority of His ambassadors. They serve as signs that point people to the Kingdom.

> ***Example:*** A missionary in a remote area prays for rain during a drought, and the miraculous provision leads an entire village to faith.

The Pitfalls of Misusing Authority

Self-Glorification

Authority is not for personal recognition or gain. Ambassadors must redirect all glory to God, ensuring their actions point others to Him.

Neglecting accountability

Operating in isolation can lead to pride and misjudgment. Remaining connected to the Ekklesia ensures accountability and correction.

Acting Outside God's Will

Presuming authority without God's guidance can lead to spiritual and practical harm. Ambassadors must constantly seek the Holy Spirit's leading.

Releasing Heaven on Earth

Transforming Lives
Ambassadors lead others into salvation, healing, and restoration, making Heaven's promises tangible.

Transforming Systems
By influencing government, business, education, and other sectors, Kingdom authority brings about structural change that aligns with God's purposes.

> **Example:** A Christian politician drafts policies that reflect biblical values, such as justice for the marginalized and care for the environment.

Practical Steps for Walking in Authority:
- Spend Time with the King: Build intimacy with God through prayer, worship, and studying His Word.
- Practice Obedience: Consistent alignment with God's will strengthens your authority.
- Seek the Holy Spirit's Empowerment: Rely on the Spirit daily for wisdom and power.
- Act with Boldness: Step out in faith, trusting God to honor your obedience.

Conclusion
Kingdom authority is both a privilege and a responsibility. It is

not about dominating others but about serving them, advancing God's mission, and glorifying His name. As we walk in Kingdom authority, we become conduits of Heaven's power, transforming lives, systems, and nations.

Reflection Questions

1. How can you grow in your understanding and exercise of Kingdom authority?
2. Is there room in your life for greater submission to the King?
3. What opportunities do you have to release Heaven's power in your sphere of influence?
4. How can you ensure you are operating in alignment with God's will?
5. What specific steps can you take today to confront darkness or influence systems with Kingdom principles?

CHAPTER 11

Building Bridges - Kingdom Expansion in Every Sphere

Introduction

In a world divided by culture, ideology, economics, and spirituality, the role of Kingdom ambassadors is more vital than ever.

We have the responsibility to connect Heaven and Earth, paving the way for Kingdom principles to impact individuals, societies, and structures.

This mission requires intentionality, wisdom, and a deep reliance on the Holy Spirit.

Building bridges is more than a symbolic act; it is a deliberate and transformative strategy. It involves reaching across barriers—cultural, social, spiritual, and systemic—to establish connections that lead to reconciliation, understanding, and Kingdom expansion.

Through bridge-building, we fulfill the divine mandate to disciple nations, reconcile people to God, and align the world with the principles of Heaven.

The purpose of building bridges

Reconcile humanity to God.

The ultimate purpose of building bridges is to restore humanity's broken relationship with God. This is the central message of the Gospel and the core of the ambassador's mission.

Scriptural Mandate:

"We are therefore Christ's ambassadors, as though God were making His appeal through us. We implore you on Christ's behalf: Be reconciled to God" (2 Corinthians 5:20, NIV).

> **Example:** A small group hosts a free community event where they share testimonies of God's goodness and acts of kindness, enabling attendees to feel His love.

True reconciliation begins with love. Demonstrating God's compassion through our words and actions creates an opening for spiritual transformation.

Restore systems to kingdom principles
In addition to transforming individuals, ambassadors must influence societal systems like government, education, business, and media to uphold Kingdom values like justice, compassion, and integrity.

> **Example:** A kingdom-minded business leader initiates workplace policies that prioritize ethical practices, environmental stewardship, and employee well-being, reflecting God's principles of stewardship and fairness.

Restoring systems involves addressing root causes of corruption, inefficiency, or injustice. For example, reforming educational curricula to promote truth and wisdom can have generational impact.

Reach Across Divides
Building bridges requires intentional engagement with people of different cultural, social, and spiritual backgrounds, breaking down walls of prejudice and division.

Scriptural Mandate:
"There is neither Jew nor Gentile, neither slave nor free, nor is there male and female, for you are all one in Christ Jesus" (Galatians

3:28, NIV).

> **Example:** A church organizes a multicultural festival that celebrates diversity while sharing the unifying message of Christ's love.

Reaching across divides demands humility, a willingness to listen, and an openness to learn from others while staying firmly rooted in the truth of the Gospel.

The Role of Ambassadors in Kingdom Expansion

Proclaiming the Kingdom Message

The task of ambassadors is to share the Gospel in ways that resonate with their audience, bridging cultural and contextual gaps. This involves creatively adapting the unchanging message of Christ to meet the specific needs of the people.

> **Example:** A missionary working in an unreached area incorporates local art and storytelling traditions to share biblical truths in a relatable way.

Effective proclamation begins with understanding the audience's worldview, addressing their questions, and meeting their spiritual and practical needs.

Demonstrating Kingdom Values

Ambassadors embody the character of the King through acts of service, generosity, and integrity. These actions establish credibility, foster trust, and create opportunities for influence.

> **Example:** A teacher consistently models fairness and patience in the classroom, becoming a trusted role model for students and colleagues.

Actions that reflect Kingdom values, such as providing for the poor or advocating for justice, serve as powerful testimonies of God's love in action.

Equipping Others for Kingdom Work

Discipleship is central to Kingdom expansion. By equipping and empowering others, ambassadors multiply their efforts and extend the reach of the Gospel.

Scriptural Mandate:

"The things you have heard me say in the presence of many witnesses entrust to reliable people who will also be qualified to teach others" (2 Timothy 2:2, NIV).

> **Example:** A youth pastor mentors a group of young leaders, teaching them how to share their faith and disciple others in their schools.

Equipping others includes spiritual training, practical guidance, and ongoing encouragement to help them step into their own roles as ambassadors.

Strategies for effective bridge-building

Understanding the cultural, social, and spiritual context of the people or systems under engagement is the first step in effective bridge-building. This knowledge allows ambassadors to connect meaningfully and address real needs.

> **Example:** A healthcare missionary studies local health issues and cultural beliefs to provide medical care that respects traditions while introducing God's healing power.

Contextual understanding demonstrates respect for others' perspectives and builds relational bridges that pave the way for Gospel impact.

Find Common Ground
Identifying shared values, goals, or interests provides a foundation for meaningful dialogue and collaboration.

Scriptural Mandate:
"I have become all things to all people so that by all possible means I might save some" (1 Corinthians 9:22, NIV).

> **Example:** A Community leader partners with local organizations to address shared concerns like poverty or education reform, building trust while reflecting Kingdom values.

Engage with Humility
Approaching others with respect, a willingness to listen, and an openness to learn fosters trust and mutual understanding. Humility disarms resistance and builds relationships.

> **Example:** A Christian business owner hosts workshops on ethical leadership, inviting input from diverse participants to create a collaborative and inclusive environment.

Lead with Service
Service is a powerful demonstration of Christ's love. Acts of

service offer concrete manifestations of Kingdom values and create opportunities for spiritual interaction.

> ***Example:*** A church initiates a clean-up project in a neglected neighborhood, offering hope and demonstrating care for the community.

Service enhances credibility by demonstrating ambassadors' commitment to the welfare of those they aim to influence.

Challenges in Building Bridges

Resistance to Change
Individuals and systems often resist transformation due to fear of the unknown, pride, or attachment to the status quo.

Overcoming resistance requires patience, perseverance, and reliance on the Holy Spirit to soften hearts and open minds.

Cultural Barriers
Differences in language, traditions, and values can hinder communication and mutual understanding.

> ***Example:*** A missionary engages a translator and local guides to bridge language and cultural gaps, ensuring the message is both understood and respected.

Spiritual Opposition
Efforts to expand the Kingdom often encounter spiritual resistance, as the enemy seeks to maintain division and darkness.

Scriptural Mandate:
"For our struggle is not against flesh and blood, but against the rulers, against the authorities, against the powers of this dark world" (Ephesians 6:12, NIV).

Overcoming spiritual opposition requires persistent prayer, fasting, and standing firm in the authority of Christ.

The impact of kingdom expansion

Lives Transformed
Through bridge-building, individuals encounter the love of God, experience salvation, and receive healing and restoration.

> *Example:* A community outreach program provides job training and discipleship, transforming lives and breaking cycles of poverty.

Redeemed Systems
Corrupt systems begin to reflect Kingdom principles, promoting justice, equity, and sustainability.

A government official advocates for reforms that protect the vulnerable and uphold integrity, leading to systemic change.

Communities United
Bridges foster reconciliation, healing divisions, and uniting people under the banner of the Kingdom.

> *Example:* Churches from different denominations collaborate on a city-wide initiative to combat homelessness, demonstrating

unity and love.

Nations Influenced
Implementing Kingdom values at the national level fulfills the Great Commission and transforms entire societies.

Scriptural Mandate:
"Go and make disciples of all nations" (Matthew 28:19, NIV).

Practical Steps for Building Bridges
- Pray for Open Doors: Consistent prayer prepares hearts and creates opportunities for engagement.
- Invest in Relationships: Building trust and connection lays a foundation for influence.
- Engage with Intentionality: Approach every interaction with a Kingdom purpose.
- Equip and Mobilize Others: Train and empower others to extend the reach of the mission.

Conclusion
The call to build bridges is both a privilege and a responsibility. By connecting Heaven's values with Earth's needs, ambassadors fulfill their divine mandate to transform lives, systems, and nations. This work requires courage, creativity, and a reliance on God's power.

As Kingdom ambassadors, we have the opportunity to be catalysts for change, bringing unity, healing, and hope. Let us rise to the challenge, knowing that the King goes before us, and His Spirit empowers us for the task.

Reflection Questions

1. What barriers or divides can you work to bridge in your community?
2. How can you engage more intentionally with individuals and systems in need of transformation?
3. What steps can you take to equip and mobilize others for Kingdom expansion?
4. How can you find common ground to foster dialogue and collaboration?
5. In what ways can you address resistance or spiritual opposition with perseverance and grace?

CHAPTER 12

Challenges and Triumphs in the Ambassadorial Journey

Introduction

The journey of a Kingdom ambassador is one of perseverance, courage, and unwavering faith. It is a path marked by challenges, requiring steadfastness in the face of adversity, but it is also a journey filled with profound victories and moments of divine triumph.

Ambassadors represent the King in a world often hostile to His values, navigating spiritual battles, cultural complexities, and personal struggles.

Despite the challenges, every victory—whether a single life transformed, a system reformed, or a community restored—affirms the faithfulness and power of the King. This chapter explores the dual nature of the ambassadorial journey, addressing both the trials that test faith and the triumphs that inspire perseverance.

Challenges Faced by Kingdom Ambassadors

Opposition from the World

The principles of the Kingdom often stand in stark contrast to the values of the world. The upholding of truth and righteousness by ambassadors can lead to criticism, rejection, or even persecution.

Scriptural Insight:

"If the world hates you, keep in mind that it hated Me first" (John 15:18, NIV).

> ***Example:*** A Christian journalist reporting on corruption faces backlash from influential figures who attempt to discredit or silence their work. Despite the opposition, the journalist continues to shine a light on the truth, reflecting Kingdom integrity.

Opposition is not a sign of failure but an opportunity to glorify God through steadfast faith and courage.

Spiritual Warfare
Ambassadors engage in a spiritual battle against forces that oppose God's Kingdom. These battles manifest through fear, discouragement, division, and resistance to Kingdom advancement.

Scriptural Mandate:
"For our struggle is not against flesh and blood, but against the rulers, against the authorities, against the powers of this dark world" (Ephesians 6:12, NIV).

> ***Example:*** A pastor planting a church in a spiritually resistant community experiences sudden challenges, such as illness and division, but relies on intercessory prayer to overcome these barriers.

Understanding spiritual warfare equips ambassadors to recognize and combat the unseen forces working against their mission. Regular prayer and fasting are essential tools for victory.

Cultural and Ideological Barriers
Differences in worldviews, traditions, and cultural norms can create misunderstandings or resistance to the Gospel message. Ambassadors must navigate these barriers with sensitivity and wisdom.

> ***Example:*** A missionary working in a region with deeply rooted animistic beliefs faces skepticism when introducing biblical concepts. Over time, they earn trust by respecting local traditions

while gently presenting the Gospel's transformative power.

Patience and cultural sensitivity help ambassadors build bridges of understanding, creating opportunities for Kingdom influence.

Personal weaknesses and limitations

Every ambassador faces moments of self-doubt, fear, and inadequacy. These internal challenges can hinder effectiveness if not addressed with faith and reliance on God.

> **Example:** A young leader grapples with feelings of inadequacy when faced with the task of organizing a large ministry initiative. By seeking mentorship and trusting God's promises, they find the confidence to lead successfully.

Personal weaknesses are not disqualifiers; they are opportunities for God's strength to shine through.

Pressure to compromise

The temptation to conform to world standards for acceptance, success, or convenience is a constant challenge. Compromise can dilute the ambassador's message and weaken their impact.

Scriptural Mandate:

"Do not conform to the pattern of this world, but be transformed by the renewing of your mind" (Romans 12:2, NIV).

> **Example:** A business owner chooses to honor God through integrity, refusing to take shortcuts or engage in unethical practices, even when it results in financial loss.

Insight for Reflection: Remaining uncompromised preserves the purity of the ambassadorial mission and upholds the honor of the King.

Strategies for Overcoming Challenges

Rely on the Holy Spirit
The Holy Spirit provides guidance, strength, and wisdom, empowering ambassadors to navigate challenges and fulfill their mission.

Scriptural Insight:
"But the Advocate, the Holy Spirit, whom the Father will send in My name, will teach you all things and will remind you of everything I have said to you" (John 14:26, NIV).

Before addressing a contentious issue within their community, an ambassador spends time in prayer, seeking the Holy Spirit's wisdom and receiving a clear strategy for resolution.

Ground Yourself in the Word of God
Scripture is the ultimate source of truth, encouragement, and direction. It provides clarity in times of confusion and strength in moments of weakness.

Scriptural Mandate:
"Your word is a lamp to my feet and a light to my path" (Psalm 119:105, NIV).

Daily study of Scripture equips ambassadors with biblical principles to apply in every situation, ensuring their actions align with the

King's will.

Seek community and accountability.

Fellowship with other believers provides encouragement, wisdom, and a safe space to process challenges. Accountability helps ambassadors stay on track and avoid pitfalls.

> **Example:** A missionary team meets weekly for prayer and reflection, sharing victories and challenges to support one another in their work.

The strength of a community multiplies the impact of individual efforts, creating a unified force for Kingdom advancement.

Persevere in Prayer

Prayer is both a weapon and a refuge, equipping ambassadors to overcome challenges and seek divine intervention.

Scriptural Mandate:

"The prayer of a righteous person is powerful and effective" (James 5:16, NIV).

Persistent prayer brings breakthroughs in both spiritual and natural realms, ensuring that ambassadors remain connected to the source of their power.

Focus on the Eternal Vision

Keeping the ultimate goal of advancing the Kingdom in mind provides motivation to endure trials and remain steadfast in the mission.

Scriptural Encouragement:

"Let us not become weary in doing good, for at the proper time we will reap a harvest if we do not give up" (Galatians 6:9, NIV).

Reflecting on the eternal impact of small victories helps ambassadors maintain hope and resilience.

The triumphs of Kingdom Ambassadors

Lives Transformed

Every life touched by the Gospel is a testament to the power of the Kingdom. Transforming one life can lead to the transformation of families, communities, and even nations.

> ***Example:*** An ambassador ministers to a struggling teenager, who later becomes a community leader advocating for justice and unity.

Redeemed Systems

Kingdom values introduced into systems—such as government, education, or business—bring justice, equity, and restoration.

> ***Example:*** A Christian politician drafts legislation that addresses corruption, leading to systemic change and increased public trust.

Communities Restored

Ambassadors bring unity and healing to divided communities through reconciliation, service, and the application of Kingdom principles.

> ***Example:*** A church initiative reduces crime in a neighborhood by providing mentorship programs, job training, and spiritual guidance.

Glorifying the King

Every triumph, whether small or significant, reflects the glory of the King and serves as a testament to His power and faithfulness.

The victories of ambassadors are not for personal recognition but to bring honor to the King who empowers them.

The Eternal Perspective

The Promise of the King's Return

Ambassadors live with the assurance that the King will return to establish His Kingdom in its fullness. This promise provides hope and motivation to persevere.

Scriptural Mandate:

"Look, I am coming soon! My reward is with Me, and I will give to each person according to what they have done" (Revelation 22:12, NIV).

The Joy of Eternal Reward

Faithful ambassadors will share in the King's joy and receive the reward of their labor.

Scriptural Encouragement:

"Well done, good and faithful servant!" (Matthew 25:23, NIV).

Practical Encouragement for the Journey

- Celebrate Small Victories: Recognize and rejoice in even the smallest signs of Kingdom advancement.
- Stay Focused on the Mission: Avoid distractions and remain committed to the task at hand.
- Lean on the King's Strength: Have faith that God, not human effort, is carrying out the mission through you.

Conclusion

The ambassadorial journey is a testament to the faithfulness of God. Though challenges are inevitable, they are opportunities for growth and for showcasing the power of the King. Each life transformed, each system redeemed, and each community restored is a triumph that glorifies God and advances His Kingdom.

The King, who has already secured victory through His death and resurrection, calls ambassadors to persevere, celebrate victories, and have faith in His ultimate triumph.

Reflection Questions

1. What challenges are you currently facing in your role as an ambassador?
2. How can you rely on the Holy Spirit and the Word of God to overcome these challenges?
3. Can you recall victories that demonstrate the King's power and faithfulness?
4. How can you celebrate small victories as milestones in your journey?
5. How does keeping an eternal perspective help you navigate the difficulties of ambassadorship?

CHAPTER 13

Living the Call: Transforming the World as Heaven's Representatives

Introduction:

Being a Kingdom ambassador is a divine calling that requires unwavering dedication, intentionality, and perseverance. It is not merely a role or position—it is an identity and a lifestyle. The King chooses ambassadors to represent Him, spread His message, and infuse Heaven's reality into every aspect of Earthly life.

This calling is lifelong, encompassing every relationship, decision, and interaction.

Our ultimate goal is to glorify God and advance His Kingdom, striving to carry out His will "on Earth as it is in Heaven" (Matthew 6:10).

As we conclude this journey of understanding Kingdom ambassadorship, we focus on embracing our identity, walking in purpose, and leaving a legacy of eternal impact.

The High Calling of Ambassadorship

Identity in the Kingdom
Ambassadorship begins with understanding who we are in Christ. Being children of the King, co-heirs with Christ, and citizens of Heaven forms the foundation of our identity. This unshakable identity shapes how we live and engage with the world.

Scriptural Foundation:
"But you are a chosen generation, a royal priesthood, a holy nation, His own special people, that you may proclaim the praises of Him who called you out of darkness into His marvelous light" (1 Peter 2:9, NKJV).

> **Example:** A young professional in a competitive corporate environment refuses to compromise their integrity, remembering their identity as a Kingdom citizen representing the King's values.

Embracing your identity as an ambassador empowers you to live boldly and resist external pressures.

Purpose in the Mission

Ambassadorship transcends religious activities and church spaces. It extends into every sphere of influence—government, education, media, family, business, and more. The mission is to disciple nations, transform cultures, and redeem systems with Kingdom values.

Scriptural Insight:

"Go therefore and make disciples of all the nations, baptizing them in the name of the Father and of the Son and of the Holy Spirit" (Matthew 28:19, NKJV).

Whether you are a parent teaching your children, an educator shaping young minds, or a policymaker advocating for justice, every role is an opportunity to fulfill your mission as an ambassador.

Power Through the King

The King does not send His ambassadors into the world unequipped. He provides authority, empowers them through the Holy Spirit, and promises His continual presence.

Scriptural Encouragement:

"And surely I am with you always, to the very end of the age" (Matthew 28:20, NKJV).

> **Example:** A missionary encountering opposition in a new culture lean on the Holy Spirit's guidance, receiving wisdom to build trust and share the Gospel effectively.

Reflection Point: Kingdom ambassadors operate with the King's power, not their own, which ensures that their efforts are fruitful and transformative.

The Impact of a Faithful Ambassador

Lives Transformed
The heart of ambassadorship lies in leading others to Christ. The Gospel saves, heals, and restores lives. People discover their identity as children of God and their purpose as Kingdom citizens.

> **Example:** A small group leader consistently invests in mentoring a struggling young adult. Over time, that individual becomes a thriving leader who inspires others to follow Christ.

Redeemed Systems
The introduction of Kingdom values can transform corrupt systems. Ambassadors influence policies, practices, and institutions to reflect the justice, equity, and righteousness of God's Kingdom.

> **Example:** A Christian business owner adopts ethical hiring practices and invests in community development, creating a ripple effect of positive change.

Nations Discipled
The Great Commission calls ambassadors to disciple entire nations, embedding Kingdom principles into societal structures and cultural

norms.

Scriptural Vision:
"The kingdoms of this world have become the kingdoms of our Lord and of His Christ, and He shall reign forever and ever!" (Revelation 11:15, NKJV).

> *Example:* A coalition of churches works together to provide education, healthcare, and spiritual support to an underdeveloped region, transforming the lives of individuals and strengthening the nation's infrastructure.

The Eternal Perspective

The King's Return
Kingdom ambassadors live with the hope and assurance that their work is part of God's grand plan, culminating in the return of the King. This eternal perspective inspires perseverance and faithfulness.

Scriptural Encouragement:
"Look, I am coming soon! My reward is with Me, and I will give to each person according to what they have done" (Revelation 22:12, NKJV).

The Eternal Reward
The King will reward faithful ambassadors for their diligence and obedience and they will share in his joy.

Scriptural Assurance:
"Well done, good and faithful servant! You have been faithful with a few things; I will put you in charge of many things. Come and

share your master's happiness!" (Matthew 25:23, NKJV).

A Call to Action

- Live Boldly: Embrace your ambassadorship with confidence, knowing that the King has given you the power to overcome obstacles and bring about change.

- Engage with the World: Intentionally interact with the world's systems, bringing the truth, light, and hope of the Kingdom into every situation.

- Remain Faithful: Persevere through trials, trusting that the King's purposes will prevail and that your efforts have eternal significance.

The Legacy of an Ambassador

Eternal impact, not earthly success, measures the legacy of a Kingdom ambassador. Every life touched, system redeemed, and community transformed is a testimony to the power of the King.

Let your legacy be one that glorifies God and advances His Kingdom, inspiring others to take up their call as ambassadors.

Final Declaration: A Commitment to the King

As you conclude this handbook, express your dedication to living as a representative of the Kingdom.

Declaration of Commitment:

> *I* am an ambassador of the King.

> *I* am chosen, empowered, and sent to represent Heaven on Earth.

> *I* will live boldly, proclaim the Gospel, and reflect the character

of my King.

I will engage with the world, bringing Kingdom influence to every sphere of society.

I will persevere through challenges, trusting in the power of the Holy Spirit.

I will leave a legacy that glorifies the King and advances His Kingdom.

To Him be all the glory, forever and ever. Amen.

Reflection Questions

1. What steps will you take today to live more intentionally as a Kingdom ambassador?

2. How can you live more like the Kingdom's mission and values?

3. Who can you disciple, equip, or encourage you to join in this mission?

4. What areas in your life need more boldness and engagement with the world?

5. How does the eternal perspective of the King's return motivate your actions today?

Bibliography

As Kingdom ambassadors, it is crucial to ground our understanding in both Scripture and the wisdom of others who have explored the principles of the Kingdom. The following works have informed and inspired the content of this book:

The Bible
New International Version (NIV)& New King James Version (NKJV), the primary scriptural foundation of this work.

Books and resources
Myles Munroe – Rediscovering the Kingdom

John Maxwell—Becoming a Person of Influence

Oswald Chambers—My Utmost for His Highest

Watchman Nee—The Normal Christian Life

E.W. Kenyon—The Father and His Family

Historical and Contextual References
Studies on the Greek and Roman concept of Ekklesia

Conduct research on historical diplomacy and ambassadorship

Personal work and notes
Jean-Heder Petit Frère: sermons, teachings, and notes from years of ministry.

This bibliography reflects a blend of timeless truths and practical insights. I recommend reading these resources to learn more about the Kingdom and your ambassadorship.

Final Note from the Author

This book represents years of prayer, study, and personal journey. It is a labor of love and an offering to the Body of Christ. My deepest desire is that it equips you to live out your calling with clarity and courage, transforming your life and the world around you.

Remember, you are not alone in this mission. You are part of a global Ekklesia, a Kingdom nation united under one King. Together, we can fulfill the prayer of Jesus: "Your Kingdom come, Your will be done, on Earth as it is in Heaven."

May this manual inspire you, challenge you, and empower you to walk boldly as an ambassador of the King. The journey begins now.

Dr. Jean Heder Petit Frère

www.ingramcontent.com/pod-product-compliance
Lightning Source LLC
Chambersburg PA
CBHW070045120526
44589CB00035B/2329